Encourage Me!

Inspirational Poetry

By

Gloria Faye Reida Coykendall

© Copyright 2005 Gloria Faye Reida Coykendall.
All rights reserved. No part of this publication may be reproduced, stored in a retrieval system, or transmitted, in any form or by any means, electronic, mechanical, photocopying, recording, or otherwise, without the written prior permission of the author.

Note for Librarians: A cataloguing record for this book is available from Library and Archives Canada at www.collectionscanada.ca/amicus/index-e.html
ISBN 1-4120-2785-3

Printed in Victoria, BC, Canada. Printed on paper with minimum 30% recycled fibre. Trafford's print shop runs on "green energy" from solar, wind and other environmentally-friendly power sources.

TRAFFORD
PUBLISHING

Offices in Canada, USA, Ireland and UK

This book was published *on-demand* in cooperation with Trafford Publishing. On-demand publishing is a unique process and service of making a book available for retail sale to the public taking advantage of on-demand manufacturing and Internet marketing. On-demand publishing includes promotions, retail sales, manufacturing, order fulfilment, accounting and collecting royalties on behalf of the author.

Book sales for North America and international:
Trafford Publishing, 6E–2333 Government St.,
Victoria, BC v8t 4p4 CANADA
phone 250 383 6864 (toll-free 1 888 232 4444)
fax 250 383 6804; email to orders@trafford.com

Book sales in Europe:
Trafford Publishing (UK) Ltd., Enterprise House, Wistaston Road Business Centre,
Wistaston Road, Crewe, Cheshire cw2 7rp UNITED KINGDOM
phone 01270 251 396 (local rate 0845 230 9601)
facsimile 01270 254 983; orders.uk@trafford.com

Order online at:
trafford.com/04-0613

10 9 8 7 6 5 4 3 2

Gloria Faye Reida Coykendall

Gloria's poetry has appeal in its simplicity. In it, her thoughts, feelings, and the lessons she learned are common to humanity. Writing is her way of encouraging herself. It, also, gives opportunities to encourage her loved ones, too.

Although she had always thought of herself as a Christian, Gloria hadn't found her personal connection to God until she was thirty-two. That event brought the greatest positive change for her life!

She was born a Kansas farm girl. She became a wife, mother, and homemaker for her family. Through the years, she tried a few other jobs, too, such as a telephone operator, Fuller Brush lady, tractor driver, nurse aide, postal clerk, medical assistant, and then had a small Christian book store. Gloria likes to write, sing, garden flowers, paint, do needle work, and study the Bible.

She, and her husband, Don, fished and traveled a few years. They have retired to their small town home in Norwich, Kansas. They enjoy their friends and family, which now includes seven grandchildren and and five great-grandchildren.

Gloria intends to live each day constructively. One of her favorite mottos is ...'Bloom Where You Are!'

I dedicate

my collection of poems

to my husband, Don,

for his patient support

of my writing projects

and

to all of my family and friends

for their encouragement.

Thank you.

Gloria

Resurrection Day!

Let me celebrate the day when Jesus arose from the dead,...

The Resurrection Day of all the days of resurrection!

It is the holy one, God's perfect gift of love to us!

Within this sacrificial gift,

the Son of God experienced humanity's life of temptations,

felt our feelings,... love, anger, grief, and frustration.

Jesus took my sins with Him to hell!

He died in my place, willingly!

He hung on an ugly, cruel cross, dying a death that was excruciating.

He suffered the loneliness of separation from The Father

when that heavy load of the sins of man was laid upon Him.

More dark sin weighed His sad heart than ever a soul was burdened.

Sorrowfully, but, willingly, He sank to hell

so we would have no need to go there,... No! Never ever, ever!

Three days, then, Jesus arose from death and hell... victorious!

Praise to the Father, Son, and Holy Spirit!   It is glorious!

By the grace of God, our souls can be redeemed, and rise, and sing!

We fledglings,.. humans failing,... weak,... and sinning,...

we may find our souls... clean,... free,... and flying!

We shall often be lifted by His Hand, as we look to Him for hope.

He lives; and by His grace, we, too, can rise again and stand.

+g

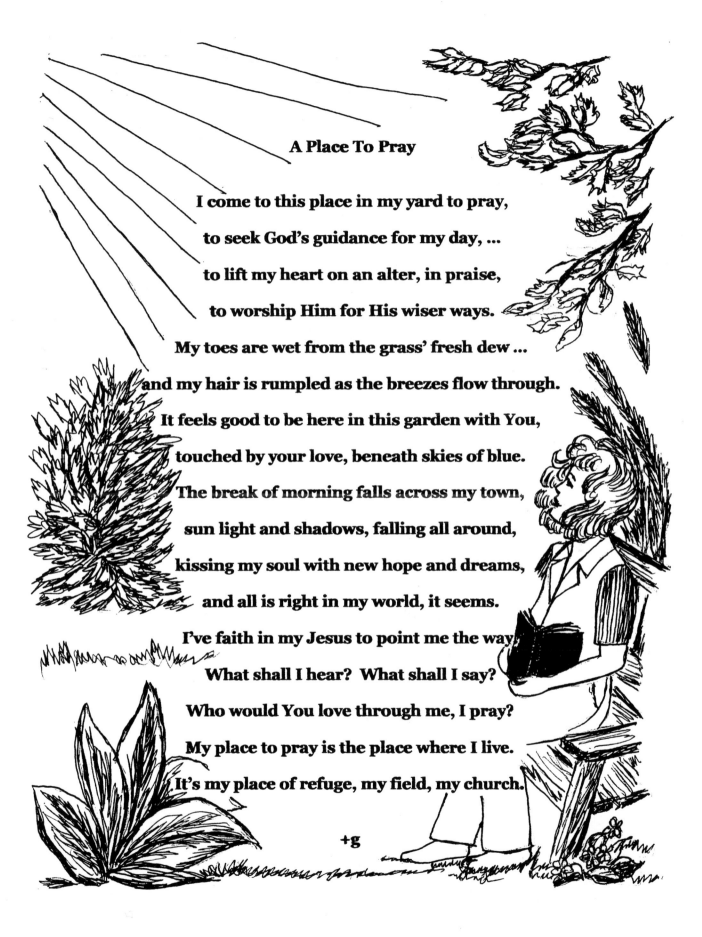

A Place To Pray

I come to this place in my yard to pray,

to seek God's guidance for my day, ...

to lift my heart on an alter, in praise,

to worship Him for His wiser ways.

My toes are wet from the grass' fresh dew ...

and my hair is rumpled as the breezes flow through.

It feels good to be here in this garden with You,

touched by your love, beneath skies of blue.

The break of morning falls across my town,

sun light and shadows, falling all around,

kissing my soul with new hope and dreams,

and all is right in my world, it seems.

I've faith in my Jesus to point me the way.

What shall I hear? What shall I say?

Who would You love through me, I pray?

My place to pray is the place where I live.

It's my place of refuge, my field, my church.

+g

What Does God Want From Me More Than Anything Else?

I am told the first of the two great commandments,

is, 'Love the Lord, your God, with all your heart,

and with all your soul, and with all your mind.'

We were born so that God could love us

and be loved by us.

He doesn't want a puppet's response:

He wants the real love that comes, freely given.

Therefore, He has given us a free will

with which we can choose to love and obey Him

or

live our lives without Him

according to our foolish inclinations.

We can't straddle the fence

between good and evil.

Heaven is no longer heaven

if evil enters in.

For the sake of love,

He made it possible for me to love Him

with all my heart, and all my soul,

and all my mind.

+g

Sunday Mornings

Sunday mornings, thank God for them,

a healing time for body, mind, and heart,...

different things to different people, near to Him, or far apart.

Sunday mornings, like a tonic, they can be bitter

or they can be sweet.

Do you like it's taste, or in disdain, do you retreat?

At times, Sunday mornings are painfully out of tune,

disturbing medicine for the soul ...

which you have brought to ruin.

Sunday mornings, sometimes denied;

"I've planned another schedule, ...

games and toys and comfort, ...

lots of time, and ... whatever the devil!"

"Sunday mornings!" now speaks He,

"They aren't for me that I ask you to give,

but, for you to be blessed, to receive, and to share, ...

to bless you more abundantly.

Sunday worship improves the way you live."

+g

Merry Forever Christmas

Christmas is a special time to celebrate

the birth of our Lord

and a time to gather with family and friends

to show our love to one another.

The end of 1999 approaches;

we ponder why we've suffered losses,

yet, because we have faith,

we rest our questions with the Father.

Blessings came by the side of unwanted things,

so we are still able to say,

"It's been a fine '99! ... because we were here to live it!"

This year will end and a new one begin.

This one seems different,

not just because we finish a century,

but, we enter the second millennium.

I'm sure it will bring world-shaking events! ...

just as the last one did!

However, crucial events will occur ...

within each person's lifetime.

There will be highs and lows, joys and tragedies, ...

like the generations that came before

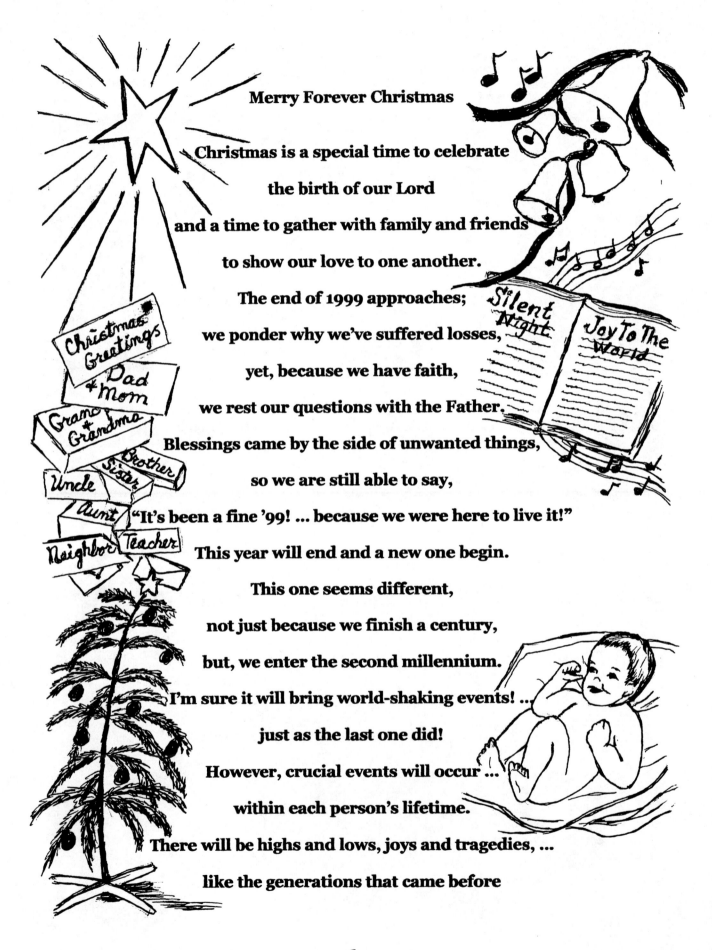

and like the generations that will come.

Although we note the differences in lifestyles,

no generation is less than or greater than another.

In every generation, in every life, ...

there are important things to be done.

Christmas is a wonderful time ...

and, so, also, every new beginning, ...

but, every day is a magnificent time to celebrate.

Every day presents some worthwhile deed ...

whereby we can make a difference.

Our Father deems us each as vital

for our moment and place in time.

Let's think how we can celebrate Christ every day ...

for the rest of our lives.

This Christmas, we wish to you a

Merry Forever Christmas!

Don and Gloria Coykendall

1999

+g

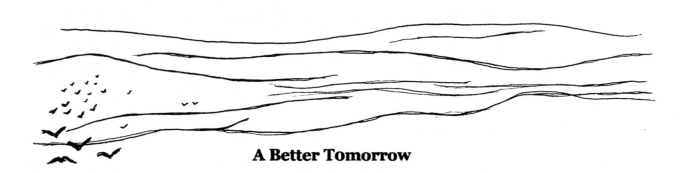

A Better Tomorrow

My life is sadly lacking,

far from what I'd like it to be.

I don't have a good education or much money.

I can't buy all that I want or need.

God didn't set me in the ease of prosperity.

I'm lacking in wealth and health, ...

someone for me to love ...and someone to love me.

I'm lacking something important to do, ...

lacking recognition, too.

I yearn for a better tomorrow

where some of these dreams would come true.

It's quite unlikely from where I stand today,

but, if I'd look into the Bible,

could it? .. would it? ... show me a way?

Would it show me a mystical formula

that I might dare?

In the past,

I've received no lucky breaks;

not I, nor anyone else

believes that I have what it takes.

I'd do anything, if I only knew what! ...

to just get a chance for a way to start!

However,

in the book of Romans, I'm seeing a ray of hope.

In the twenty-eighth verse of chapter eight,

it tells me God has prepared something for me

whether I know what it is or not.

Whatever I do today,

I can do it for God and know

that God has for me something,

a better tomorrow.

+g

Bloom Where You Are!

The Softly Fluttering Angel Wings

My angel from God watches over me

for as long as I live and wherever I'll be.

"Guardian Angel, sent from Heaven above,

if I should leave the child I love,

I thank you for watching my child for me."

I don't know, ...

did I see an angel waiting at the foot of my bed?

Did I hear softly fluttering wings above my head?

"Faithful Angel, forever near, protect me from the things I fear.

When I die, please carry me

through the blue heavens to God's loving arms.

That's where I forever want to be.

+g

Monumental Small Deeds

We're nearing the end of the year;

celebrating Christmas here and there.

It's a time for worship and gladness,

yet, frequently, we're weighted by sadness

of a world of evils, griefs, and despair.

Atrocities by humans are maiming humanity everywhere!

But! What about famines from killing droughts and heat? ...

people wiped away by fiery volcanoes? ...

smashed by earth-shaking quakes? ...

living beings drowned by walls of flooding waters? ...

masses of impoverished, ... helpless, innocent, persecuted?

In such, where is the Almighty God's mercy so sweet?

Does our Lord see the misery? Does our Heavenly Father care?

If the Creator God did not inflict it, could He not still take it away?

So much we cannot understand, ...

and we tend to blame God for the disasters to man,...

but, I think if we could see what God sees,

we would be appalled by the vast collective consequences

of all mankind's little sins!

Oh! And what about the insidious power of apathy?

Don't you know that makes the devil grin?

Let's review the great events of history, ...

all the broken treaties and wars, ...

all the buildings and burnings, ...

and all the winds and waters

that changed the face of earth.

Then, lets look at the personal ones we face.

Our hopes are great,

but our fears are overwhelming!

We can find ourselves consumed by just our living

and our dying, ...

unless, by grace,

we take this note.

Not one monumental event became what it did in a day.

It was made of little deeds, good or bad,

determined by the character of our wills and our ways.

Events were built just bit by bit,

particularly and significantly,

by both, the known

and unknown ones of us,

in the way that we have lived each day.

Again this season brings us to reflect,

with Christ in mind,

"Have I done well this year?

Isn't there some little thing that I could do

to comfort someone's soul with love? ...

to give some courage to replace a fear?

AND, ...if I don't ... or won't, ...

then, who is to blame?"

Has your heart been hearing God's call? ...

then, for the love of God, please answer it!

It only takes small acts of caring, ...

doing bit by bit, wherever you are, ... day after day, ...

just giving whatever you have to give away, ...

your heart, ... your time,... your touch, .,... your rhyme.

These small deeds are monumental

in the workings of God in time.

+g

Love, In Truth

Death came to me while I was sleeping

and I was freed of earthly ties,

rising lightly, upward winging,

through the peaceful moonlit skies.

I saw the light of Jesus shining

in the heavens, bright and clear, ...

and my heart, with joy was weeping,

just to know He waited there!

He was so glad to see me!

We had so much to share!

I thanked Him that He'd set me free and for all His loving care.

He asked, ...

"Have you been satisfied ... with the life I gave to you?"

"Oh, my precious Lord," I cried,

"Your goodness, I have felt, in everything I do!"

He asked who I'd loved most of friends and family.

With rapturous heart, I told Him how much you'd meant to me.

He asked if you were Christian; ...

I faltered there, you see? ...

"Well, .. my Lord, he's always good ,,, and I think he is, ... maybe;

I asked him not lest I hurt his pride or anger him at me."

Jill

A beautiful youthful spirit is our Jill.

We're so glad she came into our family's life.

She loved our Mike and he loved her.

She became our daughter in-law;

she married our red-haired son, our Mike.

We never expected a jewel like her.

Her personality is simple, but a little complicated, ...

rather conservative, ... mysteriously secretive.

Jill has a mind of her own, ... stands her ground, ...

but, so soft-hearted!

The facets of her ways, I cannot count,

but, they are all fair and appealing.

Jill has a passion for classical music; ...

"Oh, but, say, ...THIS girl COOKS!"

Why do we love her?

How could we not?

She adores our son

and she, even, loves the likes of us!

Jill is our treasure, unexpected, ...

a jewel.

+g

Not Tied By Things To Do

In my fantasy, as I lie between awake and asleep,

I vision myself transformed to a being of today, ...

not tied and shackled by burdensome things to do

that use up time, yet, seldom are finished or matter,

but, caught in the now, complete, with the Spirit of Christ, ...

not an ordinary lady, in small and humble places, ...

and not complicated with arrangements in mighty organizations, ...

but, simple and direct, with whom the Lord does give me.

I see me finding ladies, ... and men that choose to come,

not me as a teacher, with wisdom to impart

to persons less versed in the Bible ...

to show that I know a lot! ...

but, me, ... extending an opportunity

for those God prepared to join with me

in prayer and a Bible study, mornings or afternoons,

in camps around the country, or wherever I'd happen to be.

Perhaps, someone's life feels vacant;

one time together could heal and bond our souls

to do a shared mission,

to spread the love of God.

+g

Be Still

Some people casually walk through life;

apparently, having few struggles, conflicts, or overwhelming burdens,

but, it's not that way for me.

Even so, I'm glad to be alive.

It was good to be born a part of nature, but,

I'm happier yet to have found God and been spiritually reborn.

I've God's promise that when I leave this earthly place,

I'll be with Him in Heaven forever.

In another sense, I'm already there, because He is with me now.

He comforts, strengthens, and guides me.

When I first sensed God's presence with me, ...

when I, personally, felt His comfort and guidance,

a great weight was lifted from me.

It was the turning point of my life.

My life was instantly changed, but, it is still being changed.

I think the change won't be completed until He calls me from this life.

My new life has not been free of trouble.

Illnesses, deaths, sins, and sorrows did not vanish,

but, a change took place inside me.

I gained strength and hope when I knew that God was with me.

Now, I expect good things to come even from unpleasant situations.

God cares for my well-being and happiness,

therefore, He hears my prayers for family and friends

because they are important to my happiness.

Even now, this life continues with painful ordeals, but, I am still here!

I would never have made it this far if God hadn't been with me!

It is my intention to do good for my God, however,

I may not see the victories I want, but, failure after failure.

Again and again, I make myself sick with my struggling,

a born-again Christian many years, but, not often a joyous one,

so, the Lord lifts me up before I fall too far down to get up again.

Within my heart, I hear Him speak to me,

"BE STILL and know that I am God."

I can relax in knowing, I've sown the seeds of His love.

The clamor in my brain can cease, ... for God is God.

Shhhh-h-h   He can do whatever is needed.

He will bring the good results.   *Shh-h-h-h*

I will work because I love the Lord.

I can, also, rest and be still, knowing He knows best and is able.

He is a good God.

+g

There Is Power In A Word

There is power in a word though its sweet or it's mean;

long-lasting effects are too often seen.

There is power in a word; for our memories ring,

re-hurting our hearts or making them sing.

There is power in a word;

you must watch what you say;

the bread you cast out will come back someday.

There is power in a word, though its often broken,

forgetting a vow we've so lightly spoken.

There is power in a word.

You be powerful, too!

Don't listen to gossip, true or untrue.

There is power in a word; more good ones are needed

to heal the hurts, by the evil one, seeded.

There is power in a word;

choose the ones that will build;

build visions in souls

to one day be filled.

+g

Those Things That Call To My Spirit

God is in charge of my life, so
I needn't fear the future
or pine over the past.
I am free.
This is my day.
Ahead of me, the choices lay.
No bonds shall hinder me;
I am free.
What work shall be my priority?
What does God see as important for me?
Whatever it is, I can do it for you ...
because the Lord has fitted me for that to do.
He doesn't ask me to be unhappy, ...
to work in a drudgery with no song in my heart,
or no prayer on my lips, ...
with a lack of passion in my soul;
He has called me to do those things that call to my spirit.
It was before ordained
to be my life's goal.

It's not always an easy thing, nor comfortable, nor pretty.

It could cost me my name, my health, my gold.

Whether a lowly thing of endurance ...

or a courageous thing, valiantly bold, ...

something within me,

(and the same with you, too,) ...

we don't fully know, ...

just one of those things, ...

until someday,

the rest of the story will be told.

+g

(On the night that I wrote this poem, I'm sure God said to me, "You don't have time to do anything but your ministry for me!")

On The Verge Of Something Special

I know that I'm getting old and wrinkled
and slower than I ever was.
I know that I have an illness that limits my activities,
restrains me from doing so many wonderful things
that there are in this world to do.
I know that this may be all that I ever achieve in life.
I suppose that I should stop dreaming my fantasies
of great needs that I might meet, ...
of opportunities where I might live and give
a testimony for my God.
I've done a few things that were fruitful.
What I did, I thought were preparations to begin
the real work that was to be done.
I think what I set out to do, I've fallen so short, but,
I still have an incurable!   ... or undying faith! ...
that even now, in my old age, there is a war to wage.
There is something that the Lord says must be done
and it must be done by me.
That is so, only because of His love for me,
for as His child, He has a delight in me.

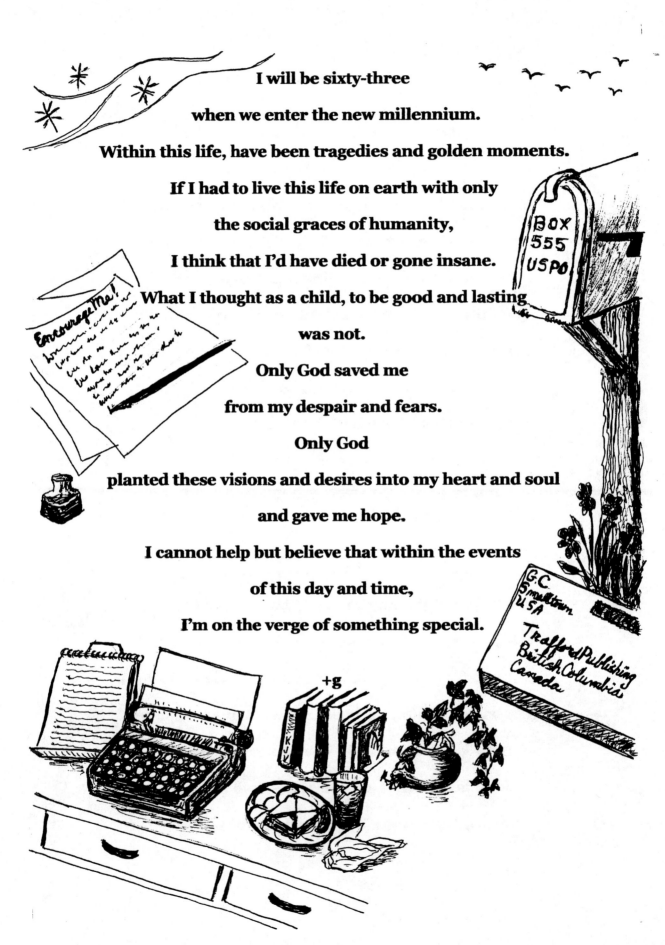

I will be sixty-three
when we enter the new millennium.
Within this life, have been tragedies and golden moments.
If I had to live this life on earth with only
the social graces of humanity,
I think that I'd have died or gone insane.
What I thought as a child, to be good and lasting
was not.
Only God saved me
from my despair and fears.
Only God
planted these visions and desires into my heart and soul
and gave me hope.
I cannot help but believe that within the events
of this day and time,
I'm on the verge of something special.

The Great Storm Is Over

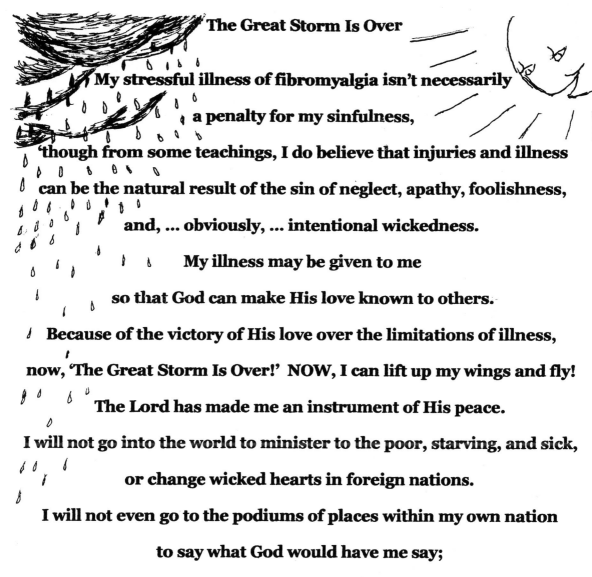

My stressful illness of fibromyalgia isn't necessarily

a penalty for my sinfulness,

'though from some teachings, I do believe that injuries and illness

can be the natural result of the sin of neglect, apathy, foolishness,

and, ... obviously, ... intentional wickedness.

My illness may be given to me

so that God can make His love known to others.

Because of the victory of His love over the limitations of illness,

now, 'The Great Storm Is Over!' NOW, I can lift up my wings and fly!

The Lord has made me an instrument of His peace.

I will not go into the world to minister to the poor, starving, and sick,

or change wicked hearts in foreign nations.

I will not even go to the podiums of places within my own nation

to say what God would have me say;

I can tell my world of loved ones, friends, neighbors, and strangers,

what God has done for me ..AND .. I can tell it from my headquarters.

I can tell it in my mission field.

What I do, I can and will do from my home ...or wherever I am.

As I have been touched, I will touch.

As I have been given, I will give.

+g

A Conflicted Spirit

I've turned off the TV sermons

to receive from Holy Spirit within my soul.

I regret the drift of our present Sunday lifestyle.

This isn't what I had in mind when I decided to be a free Christian.

God is still very present,

but, we aren't always as aware of Him.

Sundays are beginning to be like ordinary days of the week.

The Lord deserves more from me than this.

It isn't that I think regular church attendance

is most important to Him,

but, that it's a stabilizing, strengthening, renewing force for me.

What God wants from me most isn't my presence in a pew.

He does not wish me to be in the earthly congregation

every time the building's doors are opened.

There need not be guilt in me for being inadequate and imperfect.

I am redeemed, ... washed in His blood, ... clean in His eyes, ...

still I search and strain to know and achieve the purpose of my life.

I've missed the mark again; time is growing shorter.

Yes, I've heard the preacher preach,

"Be, ... instead of worrying about 'do'."

I believe and I agree, but I don't believe it's quite enough.

What I feel about 'being' versus 'doing'

is a matter of perspective and balance.

To one extreme or the other, I'll miss Him, won't I?

Praise God, by His grace, I'm saved 'though I do nothing well!

Yet, am I not saved by His grace to 'do' if I can?

Perhaps this 'if I can' is a partial answer.

Limitations come in many disguises.

Some good, sweet Christians recognize nothing in themselves

for serving.

I see so many opportunities and potentials

that I can't choose one way and commit myself to it.

What I have achieved with the years God has given me

may have been done according to God's design,

but, I feel I have failed, ... fallen short!

I've not found the ministry while there is time to do it.

I'm confused about the combination of spiritual things

and earthly things.

Why do daily things of this physical realm so get in the way

of the work I feel called to do?

The writing seems so important!

I can't think the writing is not His Creation in me!

I could have used my music more effectively,

but, now my best voice has gone, ...

gone ...

without doing what it was supposed to have done!

I see, also, the part of me that paints visions...

to which others seem to relate

and appreciate.

Will that part, also, wane, ... be unfulfilled?

How can I let it live in my life alongside the words in my soul?

And ... the remains of my songs, ...

How can each receive it's due

when there is so little of me?

My days are stolen from becoming those things

by the sickness in me, ...

by the tending of earthly things that are mundane,

but, very necessary.

My strength and time can't stretch far enough for all.

So much time is spent tending the physical needs

instead of nurturing the spiritual.

No matter! I CANNOT stop 'care-taking'

although, I yearn to soar in the Spirit, ...

because, to neglect the physical needs of the world,

I'd negate the purity of my work for His love.

It should not be one without the other.

It cannot be.

I must find balance.

I must use wisdom; ...

be able to say 'No' or 'Not now' or 'Later.'

I must not feel so compelled to please mankind,

but, be willing to be judged by them unjustly,

while I displease them in my efforts to please God.

For today, Lord,

let me count this meditation as my ministry for You.

Let me find a singleness of vision ...

and be successful within each day's work,

whatever it is that I do.

+g

Soul Winners

Like my brothers and sisters, I admired those few

with special talents to witness for You,

thinking I had little that I could do,

thinking it took more than my little mind knew,

but,

what if I did speak to one each day,

touched someone in Christ's loving way?

a greater price, be willing to pay, ...

face my fears of rejection, of being turned away?

What if I were willing to endure such pain

time and again for perhaps one gain?

An easier road, my Lord would not ordain,

considering my soul, which He died to attain!

The possibility of the joys ahead

overcomes my cowardly fears and dread.

"If I'd gain one soul per month," I said, ...

(The souls were multiplying rapidly in my head!)

a full time work every day of the week,

I would many times fail for the souls I seek.

A failure percent of ninety-six looks less bleak

if you could realize for a year, ... a twelve soul peak!

JANUARY — I find you. We are 2 Soul Winners!

FEBRUARY — I find one — You find one! We are now 4!

MARCH — 4 find 4 Now we're 8!

APRIL — 8 souls win 8 souls = 16 SOULS

MAY — 16 gain 16 = 32 Souls!

JUNE — 32 Soul winners gain 32 Soul winners, 64 Souls!

JULY — 64 + 64 = 128 Souls for Christ

AUGUST — 128 Soldiers of God recruit another 128 Souls for the Army of God.

SEPTEMBER — 256 + 256 / 512 Souls

OCTOBER — 512 +g / ?

NOVEMBER — 1024 + 1024 / 2048 Born of the Spirit

DECEMBER — 2048 + 2048 / 4096! Praise God!

If I live long, how many could I see?

Counting the possibilities boggles me!

Oh, Good Gracious! More than that could be!

If those souls were soul winners,

then, what could that be?

I help one soul per month to find their Savior,

then help that soul to become a soul winner,

who would aim as I do

to gain another soul winner per month

who would, also, teach soul winners to do the same,

In ONE YEAR'S TIME,

Four thousand ninety-six souls are a possibility!

Proof of our success in saving souls

isn't something earthly eyes and minds surely see,

so we can't count people's souls like apples.

Faith will be used diligently.

This isn't part of our lives, physically.

It's something we'll see in Heaven, spiritually.

Praise God!

Homecoming

It's a yearly event often missed, ... so many cares in this world;

valid sickness or important business, ... life's many true crises, ...

but, often, ... it's my mood in a twist!

At least, this year I'll be there.

I'll have one more time with those still here

before they slip out of this life into the Great Somewhere,

faces from the past, no longer connected with me.

Homecoming interrupts my haste, haunts me with my youthful folly,

revives my regret of shameful waste.

Now our fathers are gone,

and Mama, too, has past away.

All we have left, a few jewels and a golden one.

There is my aunt!

There's a friend from so far!

Yes, they're feeling so left all alone.
You and I, young companion,
are now the generation, 'old'!
You don't believe you are old;
I don't think I am either,
but, sit too long, then stand;
your steps will falter
and come too slow.
God has given me some time
to re-evaluate the folks
I took for granted.
I want to do that before they ... or I are gone.
I'd like to compensate.
I'd like them to know I love them.
I want them to feel their place in my life,
I do appreciate,
just in case ...
we don't meet again
on next year's Homecoming date.

+g

Be Glad

Ah!   Remember the good old days,

and yet reach out for brighter ones.

Live each day fully and give God the praise.

No time is more for happiness than is today's.

Grieve briefly for the times that are passing.

Don't expect fate to present you with joys everlasting.

New glories will build memories to enjoy in the future to come.

If you can use today well,

you will remember and be glad for what you have done.

+g

Reconciliation

Hope *Love* *Be Tolerant* *Accept*

"Yes! ... I am me and you are you."

It helps to accept that phrase as true

as our differences often confuse us two;

for long we've perceived to know one another clear through.

Now, we've come to find that, both, true and untrue,

as, in vain, we seek the other think as we do.

Be Kind *Forgive*

Ah! Once we felt as two spirits of kind,

as our thoughts often came as if of one mind.

Give *Let Go!*

Our times together were as good as you'd find,

then destiny's winds blew us each a new wind ...

into different experiences, ... our directions to bend, ...

and changed our concepts and methods to a different end.

If we never quite grasp the full essence of the other,

Even though we talk, listen, and touch one another, ...

we may start to wonder, "Do our differences matter?

We do have interests in common, is that not true?

Could you? ...would you? ... accept me as I am? ...

if I accept you?

I can just be me ...

and you can just be you!

+g

Strength To Survive

(My major emotional battles come from my inner conflicts.)

All that life is to me...

is what it is in my head.

sewage-gray ugliness swirls like a sea;

and I wish I could stop it,

be done with this dread.

Foolishness, evil, sorrow, and grief,

have stolen my sunshine away like a thief.

In a nightmare pit

of horror and gloom,

I struggle and kick at impending doom.

'Though my life may look quite different to you,

and what you see in me may be just as true.

It's how I affect you in the things I do,

that seems important in your point of view.

John 3:16

I don't like this junk

that buries my life;

my life lies beneath this struggle and strife!

I will not die, defeated this way!

I'll kick and I'll scream 'till I'm withered and gray!

Without denial of these black things that stay,

I'm trying to find some good in today.

I know somewhere there are stairs to the light

where I can climb above my fright.

My life isn't just what swims in my head;

not the hell of the past

that howls like the dead.

My life is a spark

that lives down deep.

I have the strength to survive,

although,

the climb will be steep.

+g

The Search

What if the way to achieve what I seek isn't complicated at all?

Has noisy confusion in my clamoring mind

prevented me hearing my call?

Could it be that my human foolishness built up a silly wall?

Did I frighten myself with grand illusion?

Did I cause myself to fail?

It could be a simple balance of things in moderation, ...

some rest, a little work, go there, do here, ...

in relaxed pursuit, find my direction?

I want to know why I'm here,

and where I'm going.

I want to feel my spirit's elation

from God's inspiration!

Oh! but stop! ...

it may not be important to God

that I understand my purpose and station!

So, whether I know where I'm going or not, ...

I'll trust in my God, ...

the God of My Creation.

+g

The New Spiral Pad

I wish I had a spiral pad in which to write my thoughts.

My daily journal serves it's purpose,

a record of my life's events ... an interesting reference.

What I miss is space for feelings, ...

musing my personal philosophies,

and some pages for creative writings.

A journal of my thoughts is a record of my soul.

It is who I am.

Although, I've written pages of such,

I've yet to gather all together to make them something usable.

Continue, I must, to write my thoughts.

I need a nice new spiral pad because I'm still living,

and changing,

and becoming the being

that I will finally be.

Buttercups
(Dedicated to my daddy, Harold, ... my mama, Helen, ... and my little brother, Sonny.)

Glorious yellow buttercups,

blossoms opened to the sun,

lay low in the grass of Daddy's pasture,

where they arose from their cold winter bed.

Sonny Boy and I walked along one day;

it was then we found surprise in tiny yellow buttercups.

"Pick one and suck the honey," Daddy said.

It was a fresh, warm morning

after winter had gone, ...

when Little Brother and I found sweet yellow buttercups!

Hand in hand with Mama,

we ventured a little farther,

where Daddy led.

+g

Elusive Lines Of Poetry

From dreams, they wakened me, …

lovely, one-lined thoughts in poetry, …

and truths, profound, heard only flittingly.

I tried to grasp them in my mind,

but, impossibly.

In the hope of something I could understand,

I tried to see and let the words expand.

Clearly, they were here, … but briefly.

Now, …

totally, …

they are gone again.

I sensed their essence was Divine;

glorious scenes of nature, earthly, … and Heaven.

Could they have lingered a little while,

I'd have caught them within my pen

and on holy paper,

flowed them out again, …

each elusive,

wise and lovely …

sacred line.

+g

Where? ~ and when? ~ and how? ~

He knows ~

Forever, I am,

the child ~

of another kind ~

~ time and gain

for silver?

~ of love ~

~ in the songs of ~

In my heart,

rings

God comes to me ~

a love that heals

Prairie Daisies Nod

Innocent white and blue prairie daisies

on velvety slender stems,

bow and beckon in March warmed winds,

waving above chilled Kansas sod.

They are part of the beauty and wonder of childhood

and they still come.

Through wars and disasters,

they come.

They come though I'm wrinkling and gray,

and return every year,

in due season,

as through eternity,

they nod.

LONG, Long, Long, Very, VERY, Long Ago

LONG, long, long, very, VERY, long ago, ...

there wasn't an animal, a snake, a bird, a fish,

nor a tiny little bug to live on the earth!

There was not one person to stand on the earth!

There was NO earth on which to stand!

LONG, long, long, very, VERY, very, long ago, ...

there was not a fish to swim in an ocean!

There was not an animal to drink at a river!

There was NO one to drink water and NO water to drink!

LONG, long, long, very, VERY, long ago,

There was not one green thing growing in the soil!

There wasn't anyone to taste of fruit, ...

nor any fruit to taste!

LONG, long , long, ...

Very, VERY, long ago, ...

there was no sun to make the daytime bright!

There was no moon nor stars to glisten in the night!

There was no LIGHT to see a thing.

Only God was there,

but, NO ONE to love God!

So-o-o-o-o!

God made LIGHT, dividing the day from the night,

then He created Heaven

where EVERYTHING was just right!

Next, God made Earth with DRY lands and Wet seas, ...

and He PLANTED lovely gardens of grass, flowers, and trees.

He made the BRIGHT sun to SHINE in the day ...

And the moon and the stars, at NIGHT, lit the way.

God FILLED His blue sky with BIRDS to fly high.

They built cozy nests where they could rest in the trees ...

AND on the dry land, He put ALL KINDS of creatures, ...

like PONIES and COWS and PUPPIES, and KITTIES! ...

like ELEPHANTS and HOP-TOADS

and WORMS and CHICKIES! ...

like PIGS and SHEEP and BEARS and BUNNIES! ...

like BUTTERFLIES and BILLY-GOATS, GREEN LIZARDS,

and HONEYBEES!

When God looked at His world, ...

He liked it! That's true! ...

BUT, ...

something more was important to do!

He spoke to His SON and His HOLY SPIRIT, too; ...

(Three Spirits in One God; ... all things they knew.)

"Let us now make MANKIND to resemble Us."

so God touched the ground and stirred in the dust.

Out of the ground a MAN was thrust!

God breathed into the man the BREATH OF LIFE! ...

TOOK A RIB FROM THE MAN and MADE HIM A WIFE!

It was Adam and Eve, the first man and woman, ...

and they made their first home in the Garden of Eden, ...

a beautiful place where they could walk, ...

where God often came to them to talk.

God gave His blessing,

gave them RULE over earth, ...

said, "Take CARE of my creatures

and this earth of GREAT worth."

Over ALL of the world, our HOLY God stood.

He looked over it all and saw it was GOOD!

The next day God declared to be special and blest ...

for that was the day our good God would rest.

Now that is how our big world began;

how all living things grew to cover the land, ...

from the MIND OF OUR GOD,

HIS HEART, ... and HIS HAND, ...

LONG, LONG, LONG, ... VERY, VERY, LONG AGO.

+g

Night And Day Went

Night and day!

Work and play.

Another day, past away!

Whatever it is, it is.

Regrets, sorrows, can't change it!

A life will die,

a life will be born;

our day, too, will soon be gone.

Forget old regrets

if they can't be mended.

Walk forward from this moment, well intended.

Your dream for tomorrow,

begin it today.

You won't find it gazing at yesterday.

Be courageous; be forgiving; ...

let your tears be well spent.

You'd better get to laughing

before all your nights and days

have went!

+g

Grounded In Mother Earth

I'm grounded in Mother Earth.

She's my refuge here, a foretaste of what shall be

in my heavenly eternity.

Although I have many duties waiting here, there, and everywhere,

I still take the time to step out the door

to look upward into the ever-changing infinite skies,

to breathe deeply of the fresh exhilarating air.

Sitting myself on the solidarity of ground,

I lose myself by weeding between the plants.

I prune and remove dead leaves

and evaluate my babies' needs.

My fingers find moisture and life in the soil,

the source of earth's lively growth, ...

so, I go to Mother Earth for peace,

finding no conflict there with God.

As I sit there on the stable earth,

I am who I'm supposed to be.

I've no need for choosing some priority;

at one with God and nature

and the whole vast universe.

While sitting there,

surrounded by grasses, shrubs, and trees, ...

singing birds, hop-toads, and fluttering flutterflies.

I'm in tune with the time and season;

no need for rhyme or reason.

I'm there with a sense of timeless peace, ...

alone, ...

but not, ...

just Mother Earth,

God,

and me.

+g

The End

Today I spoke to an aged friend.

She's complained for years about the life she's in.

She pines and whines for what might have been.

I think she stopped living before she came to the end

+g

The Web

High in a corner of my dusty old barn

an ugly old spider spins hair-strand yarn;

an intricate design, quickly spit from his head, ...

then, watches intently, so still, as if dead.

How does he do it? and why? .... by chance???

Does he wait for fair fairies to spring on it in dance?

No!

He waits for his dinner,

a crunchy young fly!

It's the fly that he sees although cattle pass by.

His world is his web, hanging there in his corner;

He's out of harm's way and he's causing no bother.

Makes no difference to him when I come to the barn;

he's watching his web of bright silvered yarn.

+g

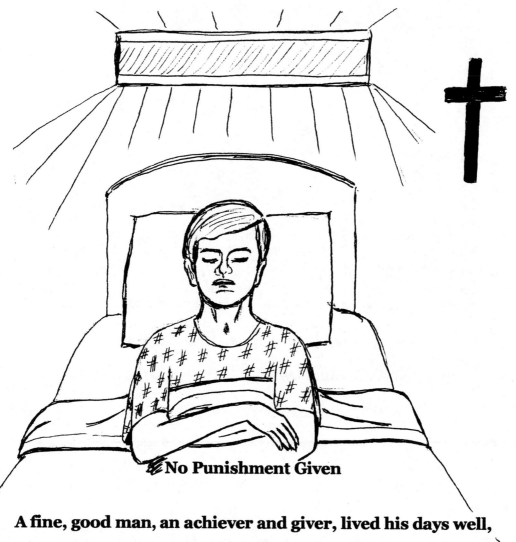

No Punishment Given

A fine, good man, an achiever and giver, lived his days well,

doing good to his neighbor.

He had no sin that had not been forgiven.

still he lays in a coma, ... so long bedridden.

Surely, ...

his mind rests in God

while his body's yet waiting!

+g

The Gift Of Free Will

Fortunately!

or unfortunately?

my Higher Power gave to me

freedom to use my will,

but,

He didn't make the best choices clear,

nor make my road smooth and easy.

Unfortunately,

temptations excite me.

Unfortunately,

I often choose them.

When I reap the regretful result,

there's no way to turn back

to erase them.

Yet, ... fortunately! ...

My Lord will forgive me;

He will guide me

and help me do better ...

when ...

at long last, I turn to Him.

+g

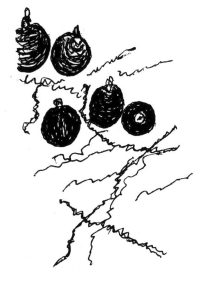

Come Alive!

Do you trust what Jesus had to say?

Groan not of your troubled yesterday.

See the sun of this bright new day!

Do you fear that trust might never pay?

Decide to trust Him anyway;

feel His presence when you pray!

Do you tire of the gloom heard everyday?

Judge not, as truth, all things they say;

hear God and with Him stay!

Do you think your God would lead you astray?

Go on, ... in love, ... His Way, ... The Way!

Touch His robe; ... be healed today!

Do you yearn to live a happier way?

Fear not some future cloud of gray.

Come alive!

Come alive!

Sing Him songs of thanks all day.

Don't let tomorrow tear your mind to fray.

Come alive to your blessings;

be glad for today.

+g

Home

A house may be grand

or old and small;

fine timbers and furnishings

ain't no home at all.

It takes love to make a house a home,...

A loved one to be there to answer your call.

+g

Wendy, Our Daughter In-law

Wendy, our daughter in-law is
sweet and gentle, fair and true.
She is honest and caring all the day through.
A loving wife ... and a gentle mother,
she has been blessed by God's Spirit
to bless another.

+g

Mother
(Dedicated to all young mothers everywhere)

Oh, my little mother, so very much to do,

taking care of love ones,

it sometimes makes you blue.

For now, talent and promise sit on the shelf

and visions and dreams are put on hold.

You are doing the same things day after day.

take heart, little mother,

you sacrifice for gain.

Look to the Lord and take courage;

rewards are waiting just down the road.

Bloom where you are;

do what you do everyday

with more flair than what you did yesterday.

Be creative.

Put some of your talents into everyday things.

Impart your talents to your little children,

and bless your household with your beautiful dreams.

The bread you put on the table

may fill your home with sunbeams.

+g

Kevin

You are my son and I love you.

You are a very special one.

You are different ... and like;

a special combination, a creation God has done.

I would love you, Special Kevin,

no matter what you'd do,

but, you've chosen well how to live your life,

as through the years you grew

from the troubled little boy you were ...

to the man you are today.

May you always feel God's love and mine;

it's there for you each day.

I haven't always known your needs; some days I was not there.

Some ways I could not help you, Kevin,

but, I tried, ... I felt, ... I cared.

As we searched the paths of our spirits,

we've survived the stormy seas.

Thanks be to God, we found our hope and better days.

As each, we looked for it, heads bowed in prayer,

seeking help from Him on our kneeling knees.

Kathy, Gentle Daughter

Gloria Kathleene, ... Kathy, ... my gentle daughter,

though no one other know, ...

for your gentleness, sweet daughter,

you do not care to show.

You use bravado as your shield,

and denial for a wall,

a prison wall all 'round you, ...

self-made to seal away from all.

I love you, gentle daughter;

how beautiful your soul!

I can see your feelings

through that mask, so brash and bold.

You blame your tender way for pain

so you seek to stop it all

by being someone smart and cool, ...

too tough to hurt or fall!

My sweet and gentle daughter,

you might as well be you;

by playing the part of someone else,

you've really tricked just you.

Although that mask seems to gain a friend,

The heart of you still cries.

The friend is cheated of knowing you ...

'till he can see through your disguise.

How many lives have missed your warmth? ...

for you've held it far from them?

Of course, you don't want to be hurt,

but, the price you pay is too grim.

How warm it is to find a heart

with whom you can be you, ...

who knows your strengths and all your faults,

and still loves you through and through!

Find yourself, sweet daughter.

Search hard.

Search high and low.

Find the child deep in your heart.

She's precious!

Tell her so!

+g

Wild Flowers
(dedicated to my brother, Sonny)

Remember when we roamed the hills, picking pretty flowers, ...

a little boy and a little girl, just whiling away their hours;

dreaming lovely fantasies, loving all Creation, ...

feeling loved and good inside, like buttercup sensation.

The season's changed now, ... time to plow, ...

hurry, scurry, worried brow;

no time for laughter, no time to be; ...

but, today I saw a wild flower, as through my tasks, I ran, ...

and I remembered days with you, ...

so, I stopped

to pick us one.

Your Steps Are Taking You
(Dedicated to our son, Michael Revere)

Dear Son, your steps are taking you

longer and farther from home.

A phase of your life has passed us.

You're free in this world to roam.

We won't bid 'bye to those dear days!

We'll not give them up; ... we can't!

Too brief, these treasures God gave us;

the cup of our life is too scant.

Time stole you away with each day.

while chores distracted our minds.

Now some tears must fall from our hearts; ...

as we clutch what memory finds.

What will repay for this robbery? Who can replace this sweet boy?

Tomorrow's adventures will sing of the days of a man, ... a new joy!

Still, by some mystical magic, let us go with you each day.

Tuck us down into your pocket! ...

We'll be elated to go along with you, wherever,

as your steps are taking you

your way.

+g

Be Yourself, Son

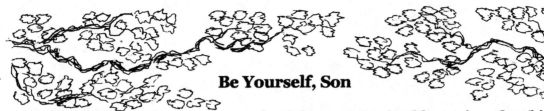

(Dedicated to Robert, my wonderful son, who had been involved in his previous years in the drug scene. He was feeling the painful loss of those years .... and struggling now to find his way into a world where he didn't seem to fit.   This poem was written many years ago. God has answered prayers and given Robert courage and faith to help him through the trials. He has a rewarding career and many friends. Perhaps, he IS a different breed of cat, but one that is a quite interesting and charming character.)

Who are you Son? What breed of cat are you?

For what prize do you run? ... what drum, you march to?

What song will you sing ... when your dreams do come true?

What gift will you bring to the Lord when they do?

You tell me your heart wants ordinary things.

You feel the late start for what life should bring.

I want for you, too, all God has to give.

Can you wait and be true? ... and in God's time-table live?

You are who you are, a different breed of cat.

To God, you're a star;

He planned you like that.

Since you are now God's man,

Satan's work is undone.

Now it's all in God's plan,

your testimony won.

I believe in your good though I know you could slip.

God knows it, too, ... holds you in His sure grip.

Don't cry for the years that seem wasted and poor.

Lay aside your fears; each day is a door.

You aren't really late; you're all that you should be.

On this very date, be you. Be free.

"Though others scorn you for your different ways,

stand tall, as a few do;

and time will bring you praise.

It doesn't matter whatever you've done, if, ...

your call, you seek after.

You'll be blessed

and one day your heart will have

a godly, joyful, spiritual grin!

+g

**The Secret Magical Powers
Of Grandma's Cinnamon Toast**

Grandma knows!

When you're feeling sort of sad

or an icky cold makes you feel bad,

you'd better tell Grandma!

She'll know what to do.

The secret magical powers of Grandma's cinnamon toast!

It will go down to the tummy;

make you feel good and glad.

With a kiss for your head, Gram tells you to wait

while she goes to the kitchen to toast the bread.

To the crust, spreads the butter

while the toast is warm,

then sprinkle the sugar and cinnamon on.

The secret is in the four-piece cut, ...

Corner to corner and corner to corner,

on a pretty plate, it's sure to work!

Grandma knows ...

and she does like to boast

of her get-better powers

in her secret, ... magical, ... CINNAMON TOAST!

+g

Crumpled Blossoms

Fists full of crumpled blossoms,

brought wrapped in simple love, ...

bring moments to our earthly days, ...

sweet Heaven, from above.

More valued, these, than orchids,

adorned and finely trimmed;

these treasures, dried and cared for, ...

respark old eyes, time dimmed.

+g

As The Seasons Go

The rain, the sun, the wind, the snow, ...

around and around the seasons go.

The spring greens come, the fall leaves blow, ...

and the winds will change 'fore the fall of snow,

and again, ... comes the rain so the flowers can grow.

A child will be born and a grandpa. die.

To one, it's "Hello,"

to the other, "Good-bye."

It's time to marry, ... have a daughter and son.

It's time to love, ... laugh, work, and play

and it's right to grow old and leave it someday.

As a child, I played at my home on the farm, ...

then, I bore my babies, ... tried to keep them from harm.

The girl is still in here 'though I'm wrinkled and gray;

It's hard to believe that I'll soon go away.

Let me watch my grandchildren ...

and understand God's way.

As the seasons go,

there comes a new day..

+g

Our Grandchildren Are Blessings

Our precious granddaughters came to stay.
How quickly our time just flew away!
Each day was so full of love, jokes, and play;
we wish that it now was our very first day.
"Cause we love one another, we have fun together.
It's not what we do or good or bad weather.
It's not where we are, at home or where ever.
We thank God for them; we praise Him forever.
The love in their eyes, their soft little kisses,
their sweet hugging arms, their chatter of wishes,
their stubbed little toes, and jeans that need stitches;
we love them so much;
bless their sweet little britches.
Dear God, hear this prayer that comes Your way;
hear the prayer of a Grandpa and Grandma today.
Bless these sweet ones of ours in every way
to be healthy and happy
and Yours, we pray.

+g

"Neath My Old Elm Tree

From hot summer sun, the shade beckons me,

take refuge awhile 'neath my old elm tree.

The quiet old elm took years to grow tall

and he's happy to stand here giving shelter to all.

Wasn't it only yesterday Daddy planted this tree? ...

now blessing my grandchildren today visiting me?

After all these years, it comes to me, ...

one of life's greatest blessings may well be a tree.

Your Heart
(Dedicated to my husband, Don. My refuge is in his love.)

Your heart is the home that I run to ...

when the world has been mean and I'm stressed.

Your heart is the home that I run to ...

when some battle's been won and I'm blessed.

No day is complete 'till I touch you

and I feel your sweet love touch my heart.

God made us each part of the other;

He joined us through love and through strife.

God made us each part of the other; ...

for always, my husband,

I'm your wife.

Your heart is the home that I run to;

take me into your arms,

kiss me, Sweet!

Your heart is the home that I run to;

because of you, always,

I'm complete.

+g

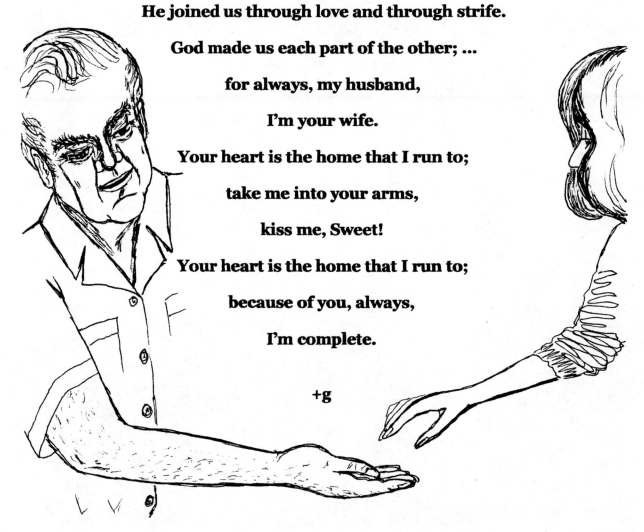

The Winds Of Life

Labored breath, wee winds of life, ... drift me far from here.

Clattering things, bright lights, and voices disappear.

Movies of the mind come flickering bye,

out of sequence scenes of my past,

just moments from here and there.

"Mama!" ... "Daddy!" ... "Are my babies okay?"

"Sweetheart! Your supper is ready.

Now don't be going far!"

I hear bells ringing! Someone is singing!

I haven't finished all of my chores, ... but, ... I must go.

One moment to linger; parting is sadness.

Loved ones I leave; my heart overflows.

As they draw near and pause,

I feel the tears they grieve.

I feel the purest love and the sweetest peace.

Preacher is preaching from The Holy Book of God.

I hear familiar voices praying;

I see the cross! .....

and ..... I must go .....

where the fair winds blow.

+g

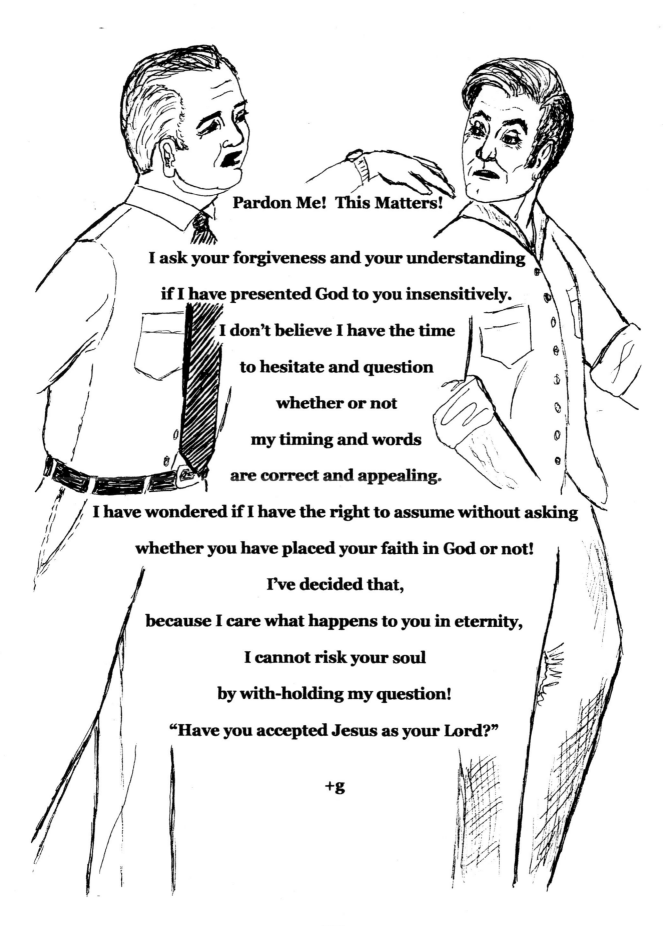

Just A Kiss At The Door

A little kiss at the door,

what does it say?

Do we take it for granted as we go our way?

Do we remember when we meet again

to express our love and share events of the day?

Don't take for granted that little kiss

and think it small importance if you should miss;

There are unspoken messages relayed in each hug ...

of how much you care,

of how welcome they are.

They feel quite at home,

like a place where they belong.

That kiss speaks of acceptance, respect.

With this gesture, you nurture character.

Does it not help to make the loved one strong?

Is a small kiss at the door just a tradition you do?

If it is, they will sense what you think they cannot tell.

There is so much you can say

when one leaves or comes to your door!

Think!

You don't know whether they'll be back in an hour

or it's possible, ... never more.

Say your 'good-byes' and 'hellos'

with your heart felt attention.

Let your hugs and kisses express your intention.

From your heart say, 'You're important to me."

Think about it and mean it!

It's nutrition, emotionally.

The one that feels valued as they leave your door ...

is stronger, wiser, and wealthier, ...

there after, never to be so dignity poor.

Your loved ones and friends

look forward to returning again

to the arms and the heart

that was open to him.

By Needle And Thread

I've never felt adequate with a needle and thread,

but, I keep on trying 'cause by hope, I'm fed;

not content to just leave the wondrous craft be, ...

for such skills represent more than what you see.

There's quilting and clothes-making, ...

there's crocheting and tatting, ...

and weaving and knitting,

you can do while you're sitting.

Grandma kept mending piled by her chair ...

to wait for the moments she could rest there.

The mountain of mending seldom diminished;

though she diligently sewed, she was never quite finished.

Mama couldn't catch up with the wear and the tear, ...

and other chores to be done everywhere.

When Grandma would come, she would often say,

"Where's me some mending to do today?"

Families are cared for in so many ways;

each care-taker has skills we all could praise; ...

but, oh, so blessed, is the curly head,

whose Grandma makes comforts to warm his bed.

Daddy's mother embroidered colors, bright and bold.

Mama's mama made her own patterns, I'm told, ...

for dresses, shirts, pants, and all sorts of things,

crocheted rag rugs, and lace doily frillings.

My mama's embroidery was soft and neat; ...

her excellence at patching, an unmatched fete, ...

but, her washing and ironing and a 'stitch in time' ...

were more important for grooming than a dress so fine.

An appreciation of art done by needle and thread

has graced my heart and filled my head.

"Dear Babies, and Grandbabies,

when my stitching is through, ...

I hope they'll remind you how much I've loved you."

This Morning

Unendingly, ... the same chores are here to be found,

however, this morning,

I stopped by my doorway

to watch how God paints the glorious skies

and reflects the colors to the ground.

As I stood, I breathed in His Being;

I became a part of His scheme.

I wanted to stay forever ... or longer; ...

Did someone say something to me?

I pulled myself inside my walls.

I plunged into a mountain of dishes,

duties to God and family, my gifts to the Lord and to you.

I don't mind the work that I do; I rather like keeping busy,

but things pile up and overwhelm me.

From the warmth of dishwater,

my attention turns to the flight of a bumble bee.

My thoughts return to this morning.

All day my mind has been turning;

some old, dubious thinking is leaving.

A freshness of heart now comes, joyfully dawning.

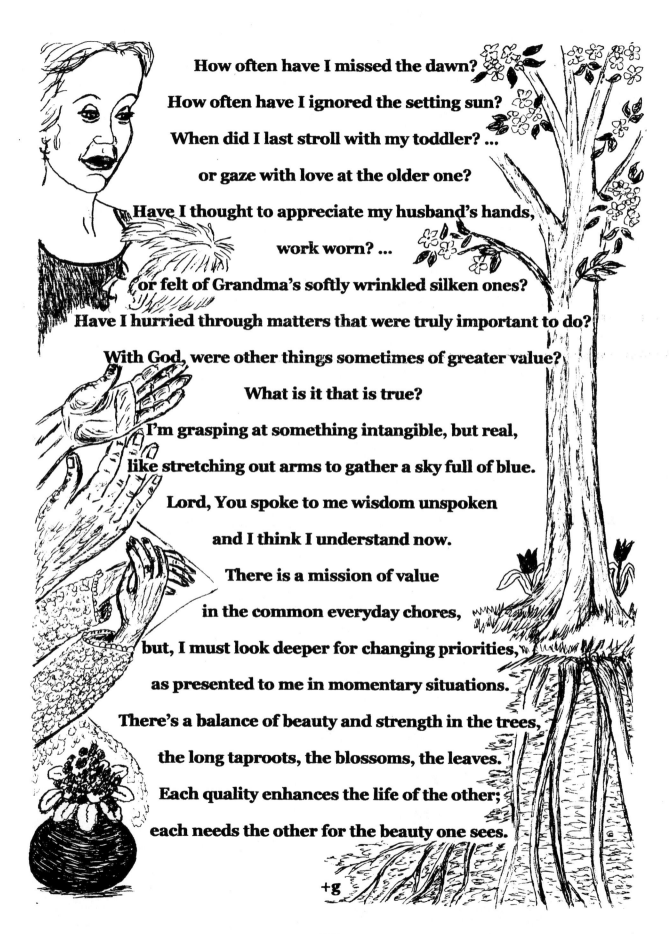

How often have I missed the dawn?

How often have I ignored the setting sun?

When did I last stroll with my toddler? ...

or gaze with love at the older one?

Have I thought to appreciate my husband's hands,

work worn? ...

or felt of Grandma's softly wrinkled silken ones?

Have I hurried through matters that were truly important to do?

With God, were other things sometimes of greater value?

What is it that is true?

I'm grasping at something intangible, but real,

like stretching out arms to gather a sky full of blue.

Lord, You spoke to me wisdom unspoken

and I think I understand now.

There is a mission of value

in the common everyday chores,

but, I must look deeper for changing priorities,

as presented to me in momentary situations.

There's a balance of beauty and strength in the trees,

the long taproots, the blossoms, the leaves.

Each quality enhances the life of the other;

each needs the other for the beauty one sees.

+g

Bless Me, Father

Oh, bless me, my dear Father,
to walk with You today.
Make me glad and happy
as we go along the way.
Oh, bless me, my dear Father,
with hearts who need your love;
make me glad to love them
with Your spirit, like a dove.
Oh, bless me, my dear Father,
with worthy work to do ...
that I may hold my head up high,
though praised by only few.
Oh, bless me, my dear Father,
so my heart and soul shall sing,
through the mountains and the valleys,
in joyous echoes ring.
Oh, bless me, my dear Father,
as I lay down on my bed, ...
with my thoughts of precious moments,
still swimming in my head.

+g

Introverted!

Introverted!

An abnormality!

I've been described in unpleasant sounding words.

In them, I heard subtle messages,

that, I was imperfect, or, at least, incomplete!

My character was defined in the past more than now,

but, I still remember!

Shy! ... Timid! ... Overly sensitive! ... Anti-social! ...

Too absorbed in myself, ... a vanity!

No common sense!

Frivolous!

You accused me of thinking in fairy tales, ...

no sense of reality!

Like a victim, my life went out of control.

I was nervous, ... depressed, ... bordering on insanity.

I saw myself in things I read

about persons with milk-toast personalities,

or a drab, mousy, little woman, ...

a doormat to wipe your feet on.

Things seemed to say, that the way I was then,

was not a good way to be socially.

This affected me,

both physically, and emotionally.

Because I believed it to some degree,

I fought myself desperately.

I determined to dig for information and insights

to correct my faults and heal myself ...

physically, emotionally, and spiritually.

I felt very deeply my own dark disappointment

of my perceived condition, ...

primarily, my ABNORMAL personality! ...

also I was angry at YOU,

because, ... as I was, you didn't value me! ...

and you didn't judge important all the things I like to do!

"So!" I thought, "So, what if I'm not the same as you?"

Oh, yes!

I recognize your character strengths and skills

are essential and appreciated throughout the world.

That's great! Be You! ...

However, I don't see what's so wrong about me being me!

You've not been treating me lovingly.

I think, if you cared for me,

you would accept and applaud my individuality.

It took me a long while to sort through this junk.

Now, I've come to satisfaction.

Finally!

I can see that some of my pain in interacting socially

was because I perceived myself as an abnormality!

Well!

Let's return to that nasty word, 'introverted.'

I'll agree that I am that!

The reason I'm not socially aggressive is, ...

'Introverted' needs time alone ... to be.

It's okay with me that you are an extrovert.

The world needs extroverts,

they make things run smoothly ...

or if there's a wrong to be righted,

they may behave rebelliously.

An extrovert can make us laugh, and entertain us hilariously.

I don't really expect much admiration from you,

although, I believe you'd be lost without me.

I think you need an introvert to do for you the things I do.

I think that here I must confess

that in my martyrdom of self-pity,

I resent it when I'm unrecognized for what I give to you.

I confess I'm happiest

when I'm doing things for me

as I wander through my day creatively, ...

when I lose track of time while involved in a project, ...

passionately,

because it's meaningful to me.

Now, when I'm brave enough,

I do my thing despite of

the more outspoken population's general perception

that what I do is mere frivolity!

Introverted? Yes!

Maybe not as much as I once was,

but, basically.

I don't believe my differences make me an abnormality!

I like what I am.

Being introverted has done a lot for me!

+g

I'm Going

Today, I will do what I want to do!

I'll not feel guilty for saying "No" to you!

I may sit, read, or stroll any time I choose;

The Great King Jesus has paid my dues!

I know what I do is a worthwhile work,

though some will say that my duties, I shirk.

I don't need today your wise approval

for God's test alone will one day prove all.

It's not selfish of me to think of myself,

to behave in a manner that's good for my health.

Some work is healthy for my self-respect

and good, clean fun brings no regret.

I refuse to live in your obligation,

falling always short of your expectation.

What I do for you is a gift from me, just because I love you;

CAN'T you see? Can you let me do what I want to do?

If you love me, ... FREEDOM NOW!

But, if you're not ready, ... I'll love you still:

but, I'm going to go my way today;

I believe this is my Father's will.

+g

Alive! Alive! Alive!

My joy is the feel of alive!

All the dreams of my youth,

all the longings of my age,

still I look for that life so alive!

Alive! Alive! Alive!

Alive! Alive! Alive!

How wonderful it would be ...

to be always completely alive!

Alive! Alive! Alive!

Surging strength in faith, so alive!

Fight! You pitiful enemy!

Attack me, you dirty devil!

I'm strong and eternally alive!

Alive! Alive! Alive!

The treasure most treasured, ...

life lived alive, ...

In which I can work

'till my job is done, ...

while the Spirit rings in me, ...

Alive! Alive! Alive!

+g

When Will You Do It?

You needn't wait
'till training is complete
to start doing the work
that God wants you to do.
You needn't see now
the whole, clear picture;
as you go along,
the Lord will teach you.
Don't risk comparison
of your talents to others;
you'll stand in danger
of quenching the Spirit.
To begin your work,
use what you already have.
Take heart!
Get out there now
and do it!

+g

A Farmer Of Souls

I claimed a field that hadn't been sown;

claimed it in love, to be my own.

It's work from my heart, I choose to do;

the work of my days, whether many or few.

I must plant the best seed, but first I will till.

I'll pull out each weed with a disciplined will.

The field's ready to plant; the right season is here.

Over years I now know how to plant without fear.

Though I farm it with love, life doesn't begin,

'till the power up above sprouts the seed from within.

My work is not yet done though the seed's now in;

careful cultivation, I must do again.

I urge the earth gently and patiently wait;

The harvest of plenty will never be late.

There'll be a great day of joy from my labor,

when the Lord's own joy, my heart will savor.

There's no place on earth that I would rather be

than here, farming souls,

for the Lord, you see?

+g

In Faith

Some great people have done great things

with unswerving determination and courageous sacrifices,

with a heart of passionate zeal.

God bless them for their goodness;

where would we others be without the blessed Samaritans

who give hope, ... inspire, ... and heal?

I've had struggles against evils and noble aspirations, too.

I've given wealth and self to those near me that are hurting,

tried to show them some light for their way,

but, my efforts brought me little.

Those where I've spent myself most

appear to continue in angry confusion.

They don't want what I have to give.

Their ears are shut to what I say,

but, God has whispered to me to go on and not doubt the way.

As I pray for my dear ones, the Lord will send others

who may be able to free their minds of the blinding delusion.

There will be others for me, waiting, hurting, and reaching out,

with whom I can share God's blessing for us,

of what Christ's life and death was about.

+g

Moved, ... By Satan!

Some say, "There is no God."

They may say it with their voices or say it by their deeds.

Some say it secretly, ... deviously, ... in their hearts.

They've freely made this choice because they love no one.

All they want is to gratify their selfish needs.

Some of them are vile pits of darkness!

They are moved by Satan's maliciousness and greeds.

They boast of taking us by fear; they take our possessions.

They take whatever they wish, ...

but, cannot take the Christian's soul.

Moved by Satan,

the person sitting next to you, the one with the pious pose, ...

who recites your godly creeds and gives to charities; ...

he or she does so for ill-gain, ...

for social acceptance.

They say words that sound so nice!

Pity their lost souls, but beware of them,

for they've been moved by Satan.

+g

All Things Come To An End

Things come to an end before we're ready, ...

things we take for granted ...

always ready and steady, ...

things ...

or people, ...

we never quite see ...

as a part of our structure ...

so that we can be what we shall be.

Too late now,

but to thank God for them,

to hold them in our hearts,

and in our memory,

until we meet again

in our Holy Father's realm of heavenlies.

+g

When Death comes

I just heard the news, the sad news today, ...

that a friend I once knew has past away.

He seemed much too young to be leaving this life,

but, that dreaded disease struck him down like a knife.

I suppose, like us all, he felt his life would be long,

not taking death seriously, ...

dreaming naught could go wrong.

When I'm well and I'm going along just fine,

a sense of immortality on earth is mine.

I don't vision my own life ended next year;

it's my loved one's mortality that's dreaded with fear.

But whether they go or whether it's me,

parting can come any minute, you see?

A confidence of life is a joy to the soul,

but, don't let fool hardiness take it's toll.

Go for the priority today holds for you.

Who will you love?   What will you do?

Will you live this day with all of your might?

Will you be satisfied if death comes tonight?

+g

Went!

Night and day!

Work! Play!

Another day, past away!

Whatever it is, ... it is.

Regrets, ... sorrows, can't change it!

A life will die;

a life will be born; ...

our day, too, ... soon to be gone.

Forget old regrets if they can't be mended.

Walk forward from this moment, well intended.

Your dream for tomorrow, begin it today;

you won't find it gazing at yesterday!

Be courageous! Be forgiving!

Let your tears be well spent.

You'd better start laughing

before all your nights and days

have

WENT!

+g

Tired, Tired, Tired!
(a part of fibromyalgia)

Tired, tired, and tired again, ...

I am so tired of being tired!

You probably think that I'm just lazy,

but, I struggle along although I am tired.

I've a strong sense of duty,

so on, and on, and on, I plod.

I couldn't sleep for hours last night;

no pills or other tricks worked for my plight.

Dull body aches from head to toe;

nerves aggravate their way through the spinal flow,

Then, finally, I sleep, blessed numb sleep.

For daytime activity, I can usually inspire myself

just enough to keep myself going,

but, sometimes, I get so angry about having no control

of this ridiculously unbelievable syndrome;

I get emotionally defensive, and I feel mean!

This abnormality

makes me feel so depressed and low,

that to be courteous to you is all I can do.

I guess it's nice that you feel chipper,

but, ... please, for a little while,

don't do it with me too much.

I'm sorry to say that today

I don't think your jokes are so funny.

Another day, I may feel able,

to fake a pleasant personality.

I hope tomorrow I'll feel better,

and I will sincerely be myself,

which you might find to be

a pleasant and friendly lady.

However, today,

I'm just a fake

for harmony's sake.

+g

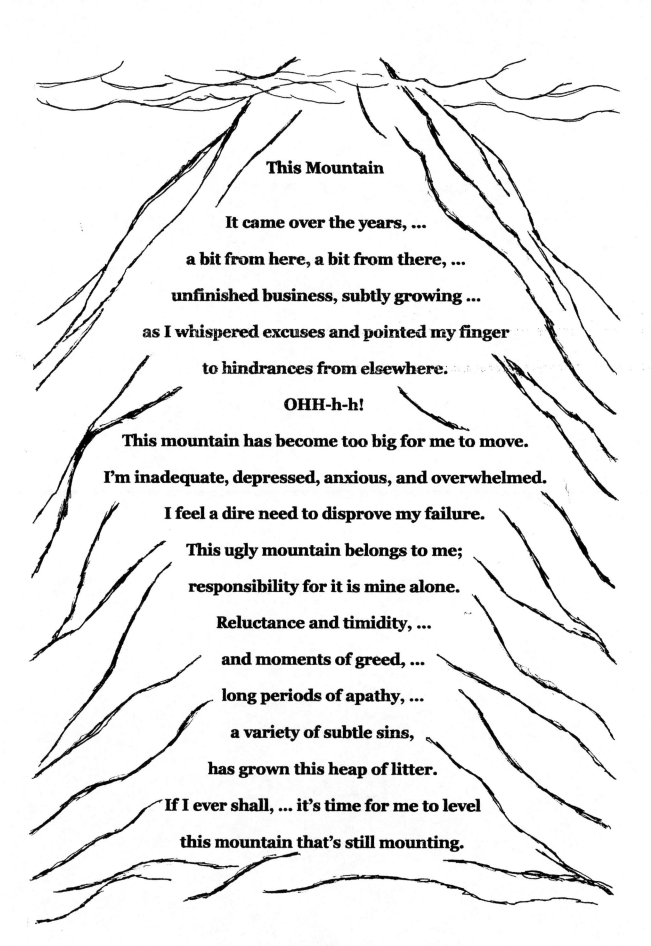

This Mountain

It came over the years, ...

a bit from here, a bit from there, ...

unfinished business, subtly growing ...

as I whispered excuses and pointed my finger

to hindrances from elsewhere.

OHH-h-h!

This mountain has become too big for me to move.

I'm inadequate, depressed, anxious, and overwhelmed.

I feel a dire need to disprove my failure.

This ugly mountain belongs to me;

responsibility for it is mine alone.

Reluctance and timidity, ...

and moments of greed, ...

long periods of apathy, ...

a variety of subtle sins,

has grown this heap of litter.

If I ever shall, ... it's time for me to level

this mountain that's still mounting.

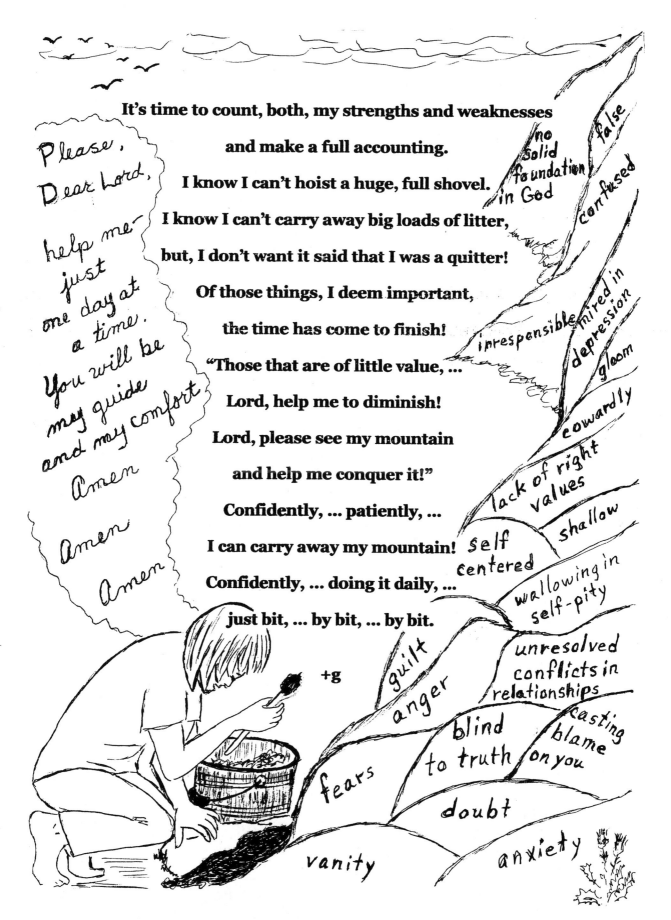

The Unused Talent

The unused talent, ...

will it be missed by the world?

Could someone have benefited by that talent unfurled?

God gave me a talent that's such fun to do, but,

I've held it back for spare times that are few.

I'm a capable person that can do a lot, ...

so day to day, in other chores, I'm caught.

I want to do right by God and man,

to do the best in this life that I can.

Many care-taking chores and wants to fill, ...

all good works to do, ...can they fill my bill?

Can I go to the Lord, say I didn't find time? ...

to sing you a song, paint pictures, or write rhyme?

My gift isn't so great for the world to miss.

Yes, the world could live quite well without this!

Yet, if I take the chance to enjoy and share it,

my frivolous talent may brighten a spirit!

This matter concerns, both me, and the Lord; ...

might I die unfinished, ... feeling anguished grief, cry?

Could I look at Jesus if I won't even try?

XXOO   +g

Which Way?

When hard times call for decisions,

the mind fights for light through the dark.

Which way shall I go for the right way?

What doom lurks beyond the wrong way?

No light has directed the path I should walk.

Why has the Lord been so silent? Does He not know I'm afraid?

Does He not know the pain I foresee wherever from doom I flee?

I've used all my knowledge to the best of my skill, ...

all the Lord's given me to work for His will.

I've stared at this problem, both this way and that; ...

I'm whirling in circles, "Where am I at?"

I trust the Lord's wisdom; I want to do what He wants,

IF I can but understand what it IS that He wants!

All will be well when the Lord's will is done ...

for He sees the way clearly to each victory won.

Have I judged each way by His Holy Word?

Did I hear the Lord say some ways would be wrong?

Was the Lord strangely silent to point my way?

Perhaps, my direction isn't on this day important to God

and He will bless me for working wherever my feet shall trod!

+g

My Fault or God's Decree?

I didn't get what I wanted.

I didn't get what I was determined to get.

I wanted to live my life vividly, ... abundantly.

I knew things were wrong that should be changed.

My life was in chaos, but I knew God cared.

God could teach me better ways; ...

He would take me with Him!

There would be prayers answered ...

and I thought that when they were,

I would be free to soar like the eagle, ...

sing to my heart's content, ...

I could laugh, love, and embrace people.

I would not be deceived by sin.

Shackles would not bind me.

Life would be thrilling and vital, ...

new things to explore, everyday an adventure!

Old talents would become more prolific, ...

but, not!

Quite surely my faith in God was rewarded;

prayers were answered;

all my life was changed ...except my health!

I wonder why.

Was it my fault? .... or God's decree?

Fibromyalgia,

so subtle and mysterious,

has narrowed my world,

made my struggle frequent,

and my achievements short,

and changed my sense of adventure.

I wonder;

was it my fault?

or ...

was it God's decree? ...

that made my road

a more narrow one

for me?

+g

Fizzled Out

Started out yesterday chipper and bright,

but, going today is more of a fight.

Met a late-in-the-day crisis that caused great stress

and the stress turned well-being into quite a mess.

To meet each day's challenge to fill a need,

fills me with purpose for a worthwhile deed.

I wish I knew how to render good service

without fizzling out, getting tense, and nervous.

I rebel against my human frailty,

but, then, when I'm sick, I'm forced to reality.

It's a safeguard against vanity's hero!

It keeps the praise for the Lord

and MINE ...

down

to

ZERO!

+g

Dear Megan Marie

Dear Megan Marie, full of love and thought, ...

a tender place in my old heart,

your winsome way has caught.

I'm thankful for your fun and mischief, too.

I'm thankful most of all for the love of God in you.

Thank you to you for the joy you've brought, ...

that before you were born,

this Grandma had not.

Be forever true to Jesus

who loves you and abides always with you,

the One who can strengthen and comfort you

whether days are good or not.

And remember your old grandpa and grandma,

'cause we'll always love you, too.

Like The Desert Cactus Flower

Dear Kathy, my Gloria Kathleene,

the pureness of your spirit unfolds it's beauty like

a lovely desert flower.

Like a rare and treasured jewel,

the desert's cactus flower

opens her fragile purified petals

to give herself back to her Creator.

The eyes that are blessed

to behold this lovely blossom

are startled by the contrast

of thorns from which this glory has come.

Surely, a gardener would need to

pamper a plant with abundant care

to produce a flower so rare!

But, No! The Gardener saw the glory so pure

before even the cactus grew.

The Gardener loved this flower

and lovingly designed to make it's spirit pure.

Through the sand of the desert,

winding slowly through the roots and stem

of the rugged, spiny cactus,

constantly buffeted by the harsh elements of the world,

comes the flower, purified by the struggle

of living and surviving the pain of it.

The Gardener knew the way to love and care for

this special desert flower.

He knew that if the way was easy,

that His lovely flower

would wither from weakness

before it could share it's beauty.

The flower looks so delicate,

but, it really isn't.

The Creator has molded

and refined His desert cactus flower

with the strength of His Own spirit.

It's life fills the air with it's pleasing fragrance.

He gives His special flower endurance.

My Kathy, you, also, have been refined

by His hard blessings

and have blossomed gloriously

like the desert cactus flower.

I'm loving you and praying.

Mama,   +g

Sweet Baby Miranda Lee

Whose sweet breath is so young and new?

Who, Sweet Innocence, is so loved as you?

The touch of your skin, like a petal of rose ...

from your lovely cheek to your tiny toes.

I see you peeking to see the sun,

blinking dark eyes that light with fun.

Your rose bud mouth, you twist and twitch, ...

for tummy or dream, we know not which.

A fluff of black hair crowns your pretty head, ...

"Such a pretty baby!", everyone said!

Now what will you do when you grow tall?

Will you travel the world, see it all?

It matters not whether you win every game,

nor whether you're beautiful or sweetly plain,

be unknown to the world or gain great fame, ...

be pitifully poor or blessed with gain.

We'll just love you so much, Miranda Lee; ...

we'll be proud of the person you choose be!

We'll send up for you our love and prayers,

for our blessing from God, Sweet Baby Miranda Lee.

+g

Like Ruth

(In memory of my mother in-law, Eva Lena Jones Coykendall)

Bless me, Precious Mother

of my husband, so dear.

Let me be more like you

with each coming year.

Your life is a gesture

of God's caring through you.

Bless me, Precious Mother

of my husband, so dear.

Like Ruth, in your foot steps,

I'll follow you near.

+g

Author's note: (Gloria and Eva, like Ruth and Naomi of the Bible)
My mother in-law and I did not always agree, but were compatible over the years, then cancer attacked her after a remission of forty years. It was a difficult time for all of the family and very difficult for her, however, I received a blessing in the hours that I sat with her. We spoke of things dear to our hearts, like mothers and daughters do. I can't express how much that did for me and how I came to love her so much.

Robert Randy

Robert Randy! Robert Randy!
Dance your jig; we'll call you Dandy!
Happy Birthday, Robert Randy!
May this be the best one yet.
May God zap you on your noggin'
'till His love you don't forget!
Oh! I love you, Precious Son,
'through all your changing phases.
I've loved you, baby, child, and teen,
and now, your adult faces.
I see your precious baby face, ...
wide-eyed, innocent, and sweet;
such a beautiful baby you were
from you head down to your feet.
Your growing years, often full of hurts,
were, also, full of wondrous graces!
My pictures of your zest for life,
time never quite erases.

Oh, son, through times, discouraging,

It isn't necessarily all the fault of you;

keep seeking and seeking and seeking

'till you find the Way, tried and true.

As you say good-bye to your yesterdays, ...

don't worry, nor cry, nor fret.

Today is the day that's important now

to build for sweeter horizons yet.

I see a new face coming, dawning just up ahead.

'Though we dream, ... the unknown is fearful.

We're often overcome with dread,

but, dream on, my magnificent dreamer!

Jump into it! Risk! Go ahead!

God has filled you with much more than you've dreamed of.

'He don't make no junk!' it's been said.

So, Happy Birthday, Robert Randy!

May you dance a new jig, ...

sing a new song, ...

love with new love, ...

and praise God for His tune that plays in your heart

all your life long.

+g

Billie Jo

My beloved Billie Jo,

I don't often see you except in my thoughts,

dreaming dreams for you.

You are my dreamer, ... and a planner, too,

planning just how your dream can come true.

You're good and you're special;

God has only one of you.

You can be what you want if you work and you plan,

if you never give up and always do what you can.

Get new strength from your God

every day for the job.

+g

Michael!

Michael!

Like unto God thou art!

Not easily tossed to and fro by changing winds,

but, constant and true are your colors, Michael!

It's not yet finished perfection,

but, the qualities of Godly character within you grow, ...

your truth, your mercy, your discipline.

Michael!

As you see through the mirror,

beyond yourself, as a fragile and foolish man, ...

the reflection of God, you become.

Michael, Michael, Michael Revere!

with great honor and respect,

watching and waiting for the Lord's unfolding plan,

knowing He has a reason for each step you'll take.

With love and prayer from your mom.

+g

Yet, For A Little While

Sleep sweet deep sleep, my darling, ...

darling, dashing, handsome lover of my youth!

Your innocent, rhythmic snoring is

assurance and comfort to me.

In our weathered, feathered nest,

I try to hold this moment.

For a little while,

I caress the image of your wispy, balding head.

Our day is nearing end.

We, too, will sleep

where, now, our fathers lay in rest.

Certainly, our years can't be long.

This day, my husband, I hold sweet.

We two devoted, wrinkled old lovers, ...

yet, for a little while, together,

we warm our old familiar homey nest.

+g

Don't Leave Me

My dearest, my darling, I long for you;

my heart hurts because you've gone away.

Sweetheart, my love, come be with me;

come to comfort me while I grieve by your grave.

I can't believe that you're really gone ...

for we laughed and we loved for all time.

Now, I search for your face in every place ...

and emptiness surrounds me for miles.

Life was good to us, wasn't it, Dear?

It was good to me while you were here,

then everything stopped! ...

all too quick, ... all too soon.

The song of my heart lost it's rhyme and tune.

I'm here, but, I'm dead; ...

all is futile and vain.

Take me with you, Darling, My Love.

Come whisk me away.

Don't leave me to grieve

here by your grave.

+g

DON
husband, father,
grandfather, friend

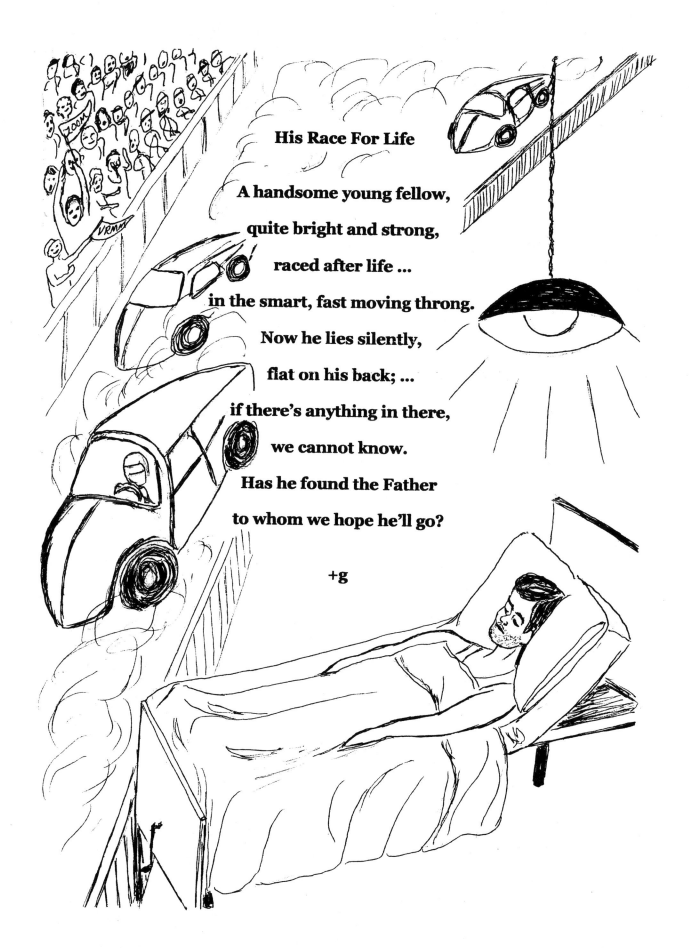

His Race For Life

A handsome young fellow,

quite bright and strong,

raced after life ...

in the smart, fast moving throng.

Now he lies silently,

flat on his back; ...

if there's anything in there,

we cannot know.

Has he found the Father

to whom we hope he'll go?

+g

The Rain

God, I'm just a little girl,

but, I know You made this big, big world.

I think of all the things I see

and I think You made them 'cause You love me.

This morning, I sit here watching the rain,

as each drop trickles down my window pane.

"Though I can't play outdoors, I'm glad to wait.

You rain 'cause You love me and I think that's great!

The sun will shine again so soon;

maybe You'll send it just after noon.

If it's warm enough, Mama might say …

I can run through mud puddles the rest of the day.

This world is full of wonders; ….

there are things I'll never know.

Your wonders are in each tiny leaf

and in each flake of snow.

For each day of my life, for as long as I may live, …

I'll be thrilled by the wonders that, to me, You give.

Let me always remember to watch the rain …

as each drop trickles down my window pane.

+g

What Will Become Of You, America?

Oh, America, America!

What will become of you?

Where are, and who are the brave Americans

who will stand for justice?

Who will be tall in heart, firm in morality,

steadfast for what they believe is true?

Oh, America, America,

was prosperity the ruin of you?

In ease, did you find no need for God?

Drifting upon seas of blessings,

did you lose your sense of responsibility?

Seeking pleasure after pleasure,

did you lose your dignity?

Oh, America, America, ...

did you think that freedom meant

you could do whatever you pleased to do?

It's said that power corrupts; has it corrupted you?

Oh, foolish people! ...

find something righteous that you can do!

Oh, America, remember! ...

are you not the sons and daughters

of our nations heroic founding fathers?

I am concerned, 'though we have good people here,

that those good may be the minority few.

I see evidence of an impending fall

if American heroes don't hear their call.

Oh, America, America,

you that have found yourselves in positions of power, ...

have forgotten to whom your commitment was due.

Are you, at heart, a true American?

How much do you care about our common population?

Oh, America, America,

a government of checks and balances may soon be totally gone.

Who of you held positions for selfish gain, ...

but, never in this life suffered penalties and pain?

Oh, I know it well; how can a friend betray and prosecute a friend?

And 'Yes', you know well they, too, will turn

to accuse you, their betrayer, of your ill-gotten gain?

Oh, America, America,

I love you, but, sometimes you give me a pain!

I've become skeptical of the sincerity of your nice words;

I don't know who to trust; for whom do I cast my vote?

It seems that once we naturally trusted those

who we thought were more knowledgeable than we.

At least, we now know differently.

Oh, America, America,

You, CEO's, that have taken your employee's pensions away, ...

are you high-society criminals better than the mafia?

I wonder if the mafia are a part of you?

I'm speaking to you politicians, too!

Some of our media are good, but, some of them are tainted, too.

Oh, America, America, I don't know what to do.

Should we all just die in our apathy?

Or ... in this great threat of calamity, will individual hearts arise?

Will there again be a common-sense wisdom

from our great melting pot of cultures

that will rise from our strong , so-called 'lowly,' humble ranks?

Oh, YES! LORD, let it be!

We have serious foreign threats, but, it is our inward sins

for which we'll pay our greater debts.

Oh, America, America!

Will your kindnesses be remembered? ...

those done by true Americans?

Who ARE your true Americans?

Who will confront injustices?

Who will search their hearts and repent?

Who will confess their wrongs

and turn to live a more noble way?

Oh, America, America,

is your corruption too much for you?

Will it be your down fall?

I hope not; I will pray for you.

During hardship, trials, and pain,

some of your citizens have shed their blood

for the goodness of what Americans believed.

Oh, America, remember!

You fought for law and security, ...

and you've been blessed

with tremendous growth, wisdom, and prosperity.

You wanted a true democracy

so everyone worked for it.

It was everyone's responsibility.

NOW!

You Americans who hold the power,

do you think you can do no wrong?

Do you rationalize your deeds as justified?

Do you think it's common practice and

that every business man must do it? ...

or, ... do you say "I'm too big, too powerful to fall?"

Remember, our pledge of allegiance says,

'One nation, under God, with liberty and JUSTICE for all!'

Those of you with huge monetary and political persuasion,

do you think you can rob the people?

SHAME ON YOU!

Do you think you are gods?

You are just devils of evil!

The truth will be made known.

If we don't take you down, ... God will!

Oh, America, America, arise!

Speak out! Let the truth be known!

Let the unrepentant ones fall six feet beneath the ground!

Let their secret sins be uncovered by the light!

Oh, America, America, it may be that we shall fall,

but, do not lose your courage, you true-at-heart Americans!

We may endure a terrible time of adversity,

but, through our trials, we will be made strong.

We CAN become a great and good America again!

We can begin again!

I pray to God for that.

Amen.

+g

A Fresh New Day

A fresh new day,

live each moment from the start.

A fresh new day,

hold each moment to your heart.

Hold yourself in this day,

not reliving yesterday's sorrows.

Hold yourself in this day,

not dying in fears of troubled tomorrows.

Will today be what you'd like it to be

as you brood mistakes that can't be undone?

Will today be what you'd like it to be

while you're focused on things not yet come?

Live well this day;

diminish yesterday's sorrow.

Live well this day,

pave your way to a brighter tomorrow.

+g

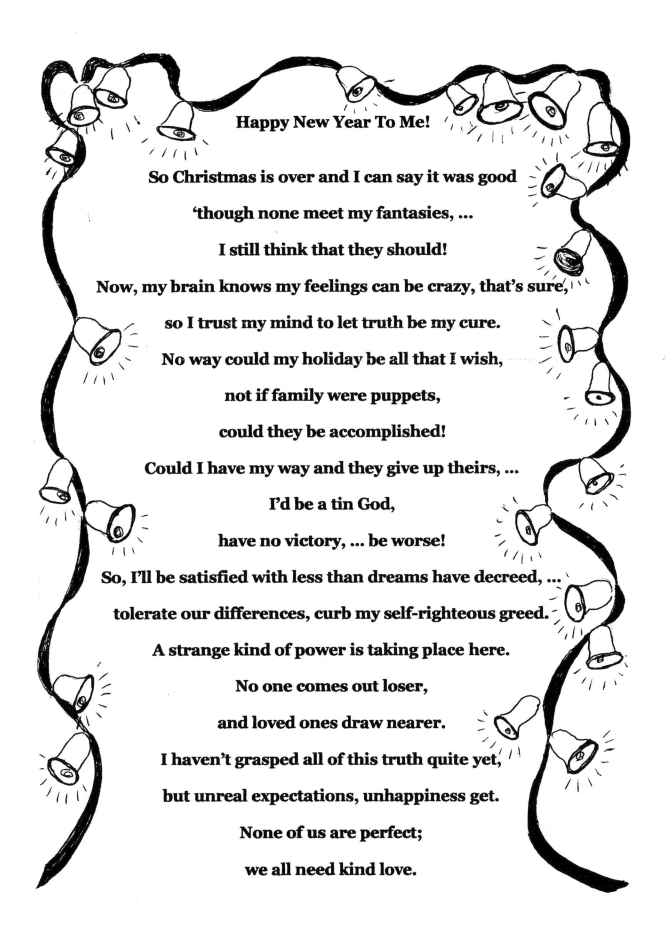

Happy New Year To Me!

So Christmas is over and I can say it was good

'though none meet my fantasies, ...

I still think that they should!

Now, my brain knows my feelings can be crazy, that's sure,

so I trust my mind to let truth be my cure.

No way could my holiday be all that I wish,

not if family were puppets,

could they be accomplished!

Could I have my way and they give up theirs, ...

I'd be a tin God,

have no victory, ... be worse!

So, I'll be satisfied with less than dreams have decreed, ...

tolerate our differences, curb my self-righteous greed.

A strange kind of power is taking place here.

No one comes out loser,

and loved ones draw nearer.

I haven't grasped all of this truth quite yet,

but unreal expectations, unhappiness get.

None of us are perfect;

we all need kind love.

It can't be all we want until we meet our Lord, above.

So, holiday depressions don't hit me so hard,

'cause I'm working on me

and I stay on guard.

To be hit with the truth sort of knocked me down.

It shook me and shifted me 'till more balance was found.

Holidays can be good as can any other day.

I can relax and feel good;

let more smiles come my way.

Hooray for my new greeting!

Happy New Year to me!

Escape

I've boxed myself into self-compromising behavior.

Self-respect is lost ... and that of many others.

My shackles deceived me of their true natures.

Such subtleties!

They pretended to be love, need, protection, loyalties.

I'm on to the game so I'm turning it off.

What steps should I take?

Break the isolation and do something just for fun.

Just for a while, I'll leave those things that hinder me.

I have decided to like me; to treat myself with sincere respect.

When someone is reciting my supposed faults,

I'll reply with a cheery smile, a long list of my likes and dislikes.

I'll sit down to call my friend whether or not I feel a need.

I might even go visiting while leaving work waiting.

I'll act like the free and independent person

that I've always wanted to be.

I'll be confident, enthusiastic, happy, healthy;

I'll have that air of prosperity,

until one day, I finally become the person I wish myself to be.

+g

This Misery

My body is slowed and soothed at long last

from the wet warmth of a long soak in my bath.

Enhanced by the blue of my mineral salts,

the healing, hypnotic water dazed the inner angry spirits.

Here in the middle of the night,

while the rest of the town rests in sleep,

I plot and plan to win this war ...

by a strategy of faith.

How glad I am for Him! ...

for He has the power to control.

He has given me strange weapons to use

to defeat the subtle schemer, who is my foe.

My mind barely flits through that possibility, ...

for fear that it might hold some truth, ...

that evil demons, so cunning and powerful,

would attack each of my doors that are weak.

In fear, I dared not look at that!

Still, now that I have opened my eyes,

that fear fell to dead sleep.

In my ignorance, I fought to correct the old me, ...

futile attempts toward the impossible,

while I dwelt on the frailties of that nature,

I was absorbed in struggle against it's mire ...

and I sank deeper into my quicksand of fear.

Days were taunted by angry restless spirits.

The hour for sleep arrived to put it to an end.

The sweetness of my loved ones was noted,

but, could not penetrate the foreign shell within.

The body holding suppressed frustrations

lay horizontal on the bed, ... finding no comfort!

The darkness chirped with a thousand crickets;

it whirred with the late August fan, ...

it hummed with the motor of the refrigerator, ...

and a jillion other sounds ... in the 'quiet' of the night!!!

There was a seemingly untamable distress in my insides.

It strained 'neath my skin to get out.

I crawled with imaginary bugs, stung with pricks of needles.

My love's compassion, so enduring, so patient, tender, and kind,

came to rub my back for me, ...

a few minutes of relief, of sweet delicious mercy!

But, I can't respond to his words of pleasantness;

I feel like a bitchy witch!

It's disgusting, for all of his efforts are wasted;

the buggies came right back again!

So, up I arose from that bed of bugs.

There is something that I can do.

I may not be able to sleep yet,

but, the body can find rest in the tub!

A few positive things, I have learned,

that the old nature isn't eager to do,

but, when the torment gets bad enough, I say,

"Enough of this stuff! I'm through!"

I can do that once in awhile now, ...

now that I've found it's help to be true.

Some relief comes in the action of doing

what I know in my right mind is right to do.

Even though the old nature is plaguing me,

a slow calm can be brought into sight,

then, my spirit can recognize truth again

and I feel and I know that God IS in charge!

The crazy madness of the deathly gloom

disappeared without recognition.

I pray to God to teach me soon

to avoid this miserable condition.

+g

Goodwill To All Humanity!

The world is in a mess;

mankind's inhumanity to man!

What can we do, Lord, to bring peace and happiness?

What can we do to heal disease ...

and wipe away the pain and poverty?

How can we resolve our conflicts?

How can we stop the wars as we have our many differences

of cultures, color, languages, and religions?

Lord, what shall we do with our fears of one another?

How do we learn to love our enemies?

We can't, Lord, ...

unless you teach us how.

Only You within our hearts,

beginning with You, here, ... where we are, ...

to them whom we can reach.

Come together, brothers and sisters!

Come together for the sake of peace and the love of God.

All together now!

GOODWILL TO ALL HUMANITY!

Jodi

Rapturous optimism danced from her eyes.

just seeing her, my heart was uplifted.

An exuberant spirit gleamed in her smile.

Her personality rang with joyful praises ...

for the life with which she'd been gifted.

Thank you, Lord, for the life of Jodi.

+g

This poem is dedicated to all the wonderful young people, who seem to have their act together long before the rest of us do, and then, when we least expect to lose them, we do.

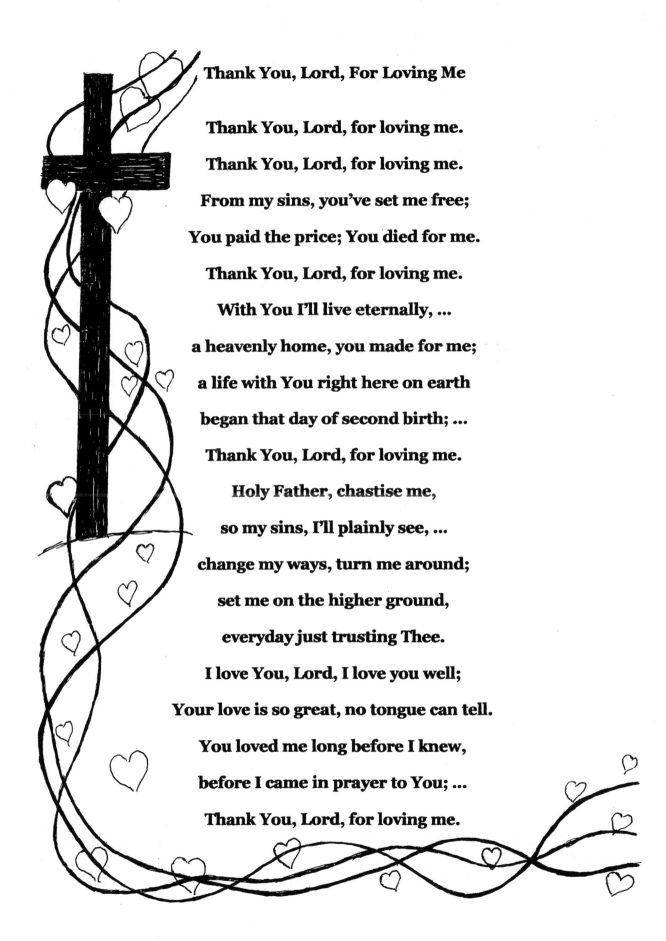

Thank You, Lord, For Loving Me

Thank You, Lord, for loving me.

Thank You, Lord, for loving me.

From my sins, you've set me free;

You paid the price; You died for me.

Thank You, Lord, for loving me.

With You I'll live eternally, ...

a heavenly home, you made for me;

a life with You right here on earth

began that day of second birth; ...

Thank You, Lord, for loving me.

Holy Father, chastise me,

so my sins, I'll plainly see, ...

change my ways, turn me around;

set me on the higher ground,

everyday just trusting Thee.

I love You, Lord, I love you well;

Your love is so great, no tongue can tell.

You loved me long before I knew,

before I came in prayer to You; ...

Thank You, Lord, for loving me.

Your Holy Spirit lives inside,
you came to comfort, heal, and guide;
joy springs eternal from within;
I'm not in bondage now to sin,
Thank You, Lord, for loving me.
Jesus Christ, Emmanuel,,
more Precious Souls, I'd love to tell,
that this life you live in me
can be theirs, too, completely free,
if they will only turn to Thee.
Thank You, Lord, for loving me.
Thank You, Lord, for loving me, ...
take my life to do your will;
Holy Spirit, daily fill.
Thank You, Lord;
I praise your Name for loving me.

+g

This is the first poem that God gave to me. It came with melody during morning prayer on March 18, 1976. I was thirty-nine and had never shown an aptitude for poetry. It blessed my soul. On April 5, He gave me another five verses.

Quench Not The Spirit

You needn't wait to finish training

to begin to do the work

that God wants you to do.

You needn't see the whole clear picture;

as you go along, the Lord will teach you.

Don't risk comparison of your talents

to those of others;

you'll stand in danger of quenching the Spirit!

To begin your work,

use what you already have.

Take heart now!

Get out there and do it!

Martha Or Mary?

Mary is praised in the Bible by the Lord Jesus,

to have been more blessed than her sister

who worked hard to serve her best to Christ.

Mary's sister, Martha, was a good woman,

not a lazy bone in her body.

Her friends and the hungry and needy came often to her door.

Martha was always busy, busy, busy; was there ever a minute

that good Martha could have done more?

Martha was a necessary person, a responsible

and charitable one; wasn't it justifiable for Martha to expect

Sister Mary to help put the dinner on?

Yes! It was a reasonable expectation,

but, Mary was drawn to Christ by something

that over rules cultural tradition.

To Jesus, it meant more for Mary to come to Him

for things of God

to fill her mind and heart with God's good

than it meant to Him for Martha

to work in the kitchen

to serve Him earthly food.

+g

A Word From God

Hear Me, you fretful spirit!

Don't waste your strength this way;

there are better things for you to do, ...

people to love,

prayers to pray.

Be still and know that I am God!

Hush your silly, noisy brain.

While you busily run in circles,

you're not making any gain.

Only do the things you can

with blessings that I give you;

no more than this I ask you.

A tired and worried mind, my child,

doesn't do it's work as well.

One whose spirit stays refreshed,

has victories to tell.

+g

I Still Know

This Spirit in me that comforts me through my hurts and fears;

this spirit in me that teaches me in my thoughts and steps each day;

this Spirit in me is the Spirit of god, come to show me His Holy Way.

He came to me because I wanted Him and looked for Him.

He came to me because I accepted Him and loved Him.

He came to me because He loves me, and what I will someday be.

He came to me just to be with me, to nurture me as His Family.

Some days I feel His Presence near

and my steps seem easy and clear.

Some days I feel Him very near, but, ...

I still must walk through pain and tear.

Some days I'm dull as rain-soaked sod

and can't see through confusion's fog.

Some days I feel alone in this world, ...

but, on those days,

I obey Him still,

for I still know

He's God.

+g

Is This My Business?

So! You are worried about something!

You're unhappy with a situation.

Perhaps it's someone near and dear to you

who has chosen to do wrong.

You think you must solve this problem before your world falls apart!

Those things could come true, ...all those disasters you fear!

Ask yourself, "Is this my business? ...

or someone else's responsibility?

Am I trying to play the part of God?

Should I get out of God's way?

It isn't your place to manage the world, you see?

Help the helpless; that's your charity,

but, don't remove consequences

when others get themselves in trouble!

Because they've done wrong, they need to feel the error of their ways.

They need to experience the results of their deeds.

You aren't doing them a favor when you take their pain away , ...

for they'll learn that you will do that

and they'll be in trouble again one day.

Step back from the picture to get a broader view.

Most times the best thing you can do

is to mind your own business and take care of 'you!'

What good have you done by fretting?

Better deeds could have been accomplished.

You could have washed the dishes

or made your family their favorite supper.

You could have gone for a nice long run

or given a lonely someone a flower.

If that worrisome problem is not truly your business, ...

or, if it is, ... but, you don't know the solution today,

then turn your mind and your hands another way.

You could make something worthwhile of your today.

If there is some action you should take

that will improve the concern,

surely, sometime your way will be clear, ...

however, this could be one of those works

that only God can do!

+g

(dedicated to my treasured friend, Virginia A., who changed my life)

For The Greater Tomorrow

We must get out of our ruts for we have a dream or two,

But, we see ourselves prevented by all the 'stuff'

we have ... or ...we have not.

We spend for wants beyond our incomes;

the bills are piling up, we've caught the sniffles,

and many other disastrous hobbling diseases.

We miss our work so often; no excuse, our boss, appeases.

Out of a job, living now on welfare,

we lose some precious dignity.

We're depressed and overwhelmed with trouble.

Will crisis after crisis always burst our bubble?

We wonder how could, ever, such as we

better ourselves to be where we'd rather be?

On this, we might agree;

the first thing is to know where we want to go.

Where do we stand in our situation?

Ask ourselves honestly where we've been.

Take an inventory of our attributes and faults

and know what we have with which to work.

The best thing we have is how we use today

to better our hopes of a greater tomorrow.

+g

Soothing Potato Soup!

This is my magic potato soup!

Its better for colds than pills or goop!

It soothes your feelings,

it warms your tummy;

you'll sleep like a baby

'till your days turn sunny.

Chop an onion and five big potatoes;

in a big pan, then boil them tender.

Add enough milk to make the soup flow.

Add some margarine and salt and pepper, too;

as much as it takes for it to suit you.

Make it hot for the sake of the nose.

Serve cornbread or crackers, ...

as either one goes.

You will be soothed

from the top of your head

clear down to your toes!

+g

Time

"Clock, clock! ...
hanging on the wall, meting out the minutes
as from time they surely fall , ...
what is this mystic power that makes us rush and run?
By what right you tick so quickly
when you know we're having fun? ...
then, let your hands move slowly
when there's waiting to be done?"
My small clock keeps a bedside vigil;
another, stately, ... guards my hall.
"Though inanimate things of workmanship,
they rule us, one and all.
"Come, now, Familiar Face, ... tell me what you know.
Why do I so depend on you no matter where I go?"
"Tick-tock! Tick-tock!
You silly speechless clock!
The works behind your face and hands tick on, ...
but, they won't talk."

John Lennon

A loving, sensitive man, ... John Lennon,

who had found peace and his place in life.

Unruffled by the clamor from various people, ...

critical perceptions, resentments, and strife.

He had faced his fears and his choices

and settled those matters within.

He'd grown through the restless confusion

and found an abiding faith to rest in.

He had, at one time, in earlier years,

been considered a rebel and upstart.

Time subtly reached into those souls

with seeds of truth from his heart.

Not great philosophies or grand sounding speeches,

but simple messages through the notes of a song, ...

of passing moments and his deepest wishes, ...

or life's sad loss at the pain of a wrong.

He is suddenly gone, ...

much too soon, so it seems.

We have listened and loved

his sweet music and dreams.

From the darkness of the world, ...

from a lunatic's gun, ...

the bullets came fast;

there was no time to run.

We ache from our loss;

we cry our heart's hurt.

Is this tenderness ended

in a grave in the earth?

Oh, this world is a vile place!

There is no sense in it!

One of God's lovely people, ... stolen,

by a sin's sick fit!

As we dwell on this evil,

the world seems hopeless and dark.

We take life for granted, then, ...

no sunshine, ... no song of the lark!

We feel angry and helpless, ...

"Oh, what can we do?"

Life is fragile and uncertain

whether we are old or baby new.

We can't hear his music,

for the pain is too near;

but time will go on,
for God's love is so dear.
Our hearts will be healed
as we live year after year.
We'll listen again to the music
and it will be a joy to hear.
The mad man's life
will soon be forgotten; ...
John Lennon will shine, ...
God's child won't be down trodden.
I grieve the dark sins of our people; ...
they seem so many and strong;
then,
comes God's light through a John
and it overcomes every sin, every wrong.

Author's note: I dedicate this poem to my son, Mike, and to all who grieve the death of John Lennon. Its often those young ones who are so special to the world that are taken away too soon, then we realize how much they meant to us. I hope we can be sensitive to the losses that others feel for John Lennon, although, perhaps he'd never met many face to face or been called 'friend'. Although he was not family, he still holds a place in many hearts.

Pull Someone's Strings

Pull someone's strings; strain their trust and respect.
You want things your way; will you like what you get?
Pull someone's strings, from their loyalty, ... guilt.
Use their love to gain power; ... love's flower will wilt.
Pull someone's strings; play the 'poor little me,'
then they'll care for you, lest they miserable be!
Pull someone's strings, ... intrude on their space;
will they, with good manners,
put you out of the place?
Pull someone's strings; you depend so on love,
but, love is one thing
you know nothing of.

+g

Using

You use the courtesy of a loved one against him ...

and flaunt your control for your selfish whim.

You betray their trust and kill their respect;

you repay them for love with your sarcastic jest.

This manipulating, that you do to your friend, ...

someday, you'll find, ... will come to an end.

You'll probably not know ... why he's gone away.

Abandoned,

in self-pity,

you'll cry all day.

You have taught this one well

how you feel about him.

The price of using ...

is

so sad, ...

so grim.

+g

Encouraging Numbers

Four thousand, ninety-six souls in one year!
One working for workers, despite the fear, ...
gains a soul winner per month
by calling those who will hear ...
who will also call those from among their peers.
Eight million, three hundred eighty-eight thousand,
Six hundred eight by the end of year two!!
What a Christian Army like that could do!
I can't figure too far, but that's more than a few.
My life has been changed by this new view.
Come with me, Friend!
The Lord is calling.
There's no wisdom at all in excuses and stalling.
Use what skills you now have
when god's love you're telling;
God shows the way to those who are willing.
Bless me, Lord, so starved hearts I can win.
I will thank You, Lord, whether it's one or ten;
I'd rather go forward
than sit still like I've been. Amen.

+g

Handwritten annotations:
- ? # !
- Pray!
- 1+1=2
- 2 get 2 = 4!
- 4+4, now 8!
- 8 + 8 / 16
- Double every month.
- Wow!
- It's a spiritual thing, — can't count them like apples.
- With faith, plant, plant, plant, — believe, believe
- The Word of God is seed!
- Souls are the harvest!
- We can't count and prove, but plant the seeds, pull the weeds, till the soil, harvest!
- Seeds planted by many may share in saved souls.
- Have godly sight.
- Know it is being done.
- Build the family for God.
- See with your heart.

Dependency

There is a pull upon my essence

That pulls me into pieces,

Varied roles with varied values

until my 'me' is lost.

I dreamed a promise for tomorrow, ...

but,, duties still call today,

postponing again the promise, perhaps to another day.

A calling to my heart of loyalties and loves,

precious hearts of yesteryear,

clinging, call for more.

They plead for just one more of my dedicated days;

today belongs to them today.

I'm tied by fear of blood in the cutting of our cord.

Yesterday, I planned to loyal duty do,

to loves which stand in waiting lines

around the borders of my heart.

Do my bit today;

Heal this urgent need,

then I'll be free and clear

to run, ... to live the dream,

in some unspecific day ahead,

Somewhere, just beyond my present reach,

I thought, ...

Yesterday, and yesterday, and yesterday, ...

and I think it again today ... although,

something says "It is not so."

Where? ... When? ... How can I reach the dream?

I cannot leave the waiting lines,

pleading from their eyes.

I cannot stand my pain of knowing of their pain.

Those hearts are used to me

being here for them.

At times they are almost fixed,

then they come apart again.

They call me to be fixed again.

I want them to be fixed!

"Be well, .. be happy, please?"

How can I be fixed and well and happy

when they are not?

My cord is tied to them.

When can I run to the other side?

Is this promise a fantasy or possibility?

Will I live ... forever ... canceling?

I seem so cruel to want to go

when all the hearts are pulling so!

I'm not sure that I will like me

if I dare to win this war!

Where is that hidden game line

where possession of me will end?

When do those loves stop pulling?

In my freedom, will their love for me die?

When shall I pull my hardest?

When can I bear to say 'No'?

When is it right to give? ...

and when is it time to go?

Either way is grief.

Would the pull bring me a gloomy death ...

or brighter years ahead?

Shall I decide to make the change,

but, then remain the same?

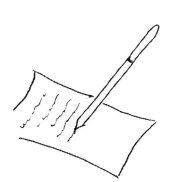

Eggspotential

The Egg,

a beautiful creation,

form,

in perfection.

No sculptor could carve such a lovely shape.

"No," no artist could create a form more beautiful!

The egg is more than a lovely form; it represents life.

Inside, the yolk holds the secret of what kind of life.

The yolk is cradled and nourished by albumin gel.

The egg, from whatever female fowl

holds potential that will never become

except when it is seeded by the male fowl sperm.

Having been seeded, the life potential begins.

It grows like magic from formless matter

unable to be seen by the eye.

Slowly, but in less than a month,

most eggs will form little eyes and brains,

beaks, and tongues, wings and claws, and other things.

Finally, a soft fluff of down covers their naked little bodies,

and somehow, after the mother has set on her nest of eggs

to keep them warm,

at a certain time, when the chick is ready,

it feels a strong urge to peck it's way

in a circle from inside

until the end of the shell falls open.

The eggshell is done; now we have a new chick,

exhausted, limp, wobbly and ugly.

The poor ugly little thing just lays there.

It's down is sticky wet.

It's bulging eyes are closed.

With gaping beak, it gasps for breath!

The poor little thing will surely die,

but DON'T lift it from it's shell!

In fact, do NOT help it crack the shell.

It's a strange, hard thing,

that this little guy must do for himself.

If you leave and return awhile later,

Your poor dying little chick will be alive and so cute,

his eyes, open wide, and blinking,

his down, a soft, dry, ball of fluff.

He'll be standing on his tiny three-toed feet

and he will be peeping his high shrill peep.

Mother hen will be defensive.

She'll peck you hard if you invade.

She's sitting on top of her newly hatched chick

and other eggs hatching beneath her warm body.

They'll be doing their pecking routine.

When the day is done, Mother will have a whole flock.

In the morning, she will slowly lead and cluck.

Mother will peck at the ground

And sometimes she'll scratch in the dirt.

Amazingly, chicks learn quickly to do as Mama does,

to find little seeds and bugs to eat.

+g

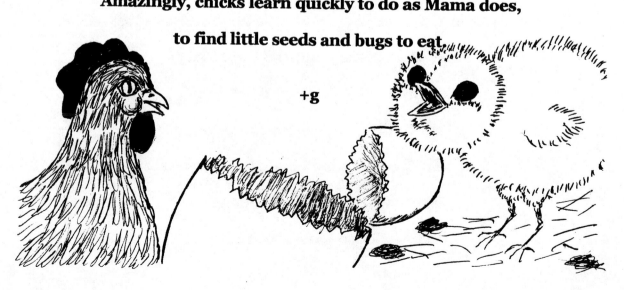

Come Here, World!

Don and I are so excited and proud to introduce you

to our favorite grandson,

the MARVELOUS,

the TALENTED,

BRENT ANDREW!

He's that tall blonde with the flashing, dimpled smile.

He's charming, handsome, smart, athletic, artistic, ...

and full of surprises and MAGNIFICENT dreams!

Do we hope great things for him?

Yes, indeed, we do!

Life is great! ...

but, it's fragile, too,

so,

for the sake of Brent,

we ask you to pray for him.

Ask our Heavenly Father's Holy guidance

in all He wants Brent

to say and do.

God bless you and thank you.

+g

Just Mama's Way

Mama was great, but, not perfect.

Now, I know that nobody is;

however, when I was a child,

she was my mama!

Whatever Mama said, ...

it was right,

it was wise,

it was true!

If she hurt me, ever,

then, it surely must be

that something was wrong with me.

Mama always told me,

"Be careful what you tell to others

because your secrets, they'll betray

when they are more another's friend

and best buddies at play."

"Your Mama is the only one that you can truly trust.

You should tell your mother everything

and keep no secrets from her

because she's the one who loves you most!"

Mama took good care of me,

especially, when I was sick.

She made me feel so thoroughly loved,

the feeling of complete security.

From psychology, now, I know, she over-protected me,

and it made me very dependent on her.

She was an authoritarian.

Thus far, in our generations, it was all we had learned to be.

If I displeased Mama, there was a price to pay.

Spankings weren't out of question,

but, Mama used guilt trips to get her way.

She made me suffer emotionally with no way to make peace.

No reason was enough for my behavior;

nothing to break the cold silent barrier,

no way to be sorry or make amends,

until she was ready to let it go, ...

except! ... to use on me some other day!

Yet, things she did that seemed wrong to me,

she would never acknowledge.

It was that I was a spoiled cry-baby, ...

touchy, too sensitive, unreasonable, ...

"How dare you accuse me? ...

I guess you don't feel well

so you're touchy and cranky today."

Mama and I were together most of the time.

She and I were a lot alike in what we'd think and do,

but, I often mused to self how different we were, too.

Mama talked and talked to me.

She told me personal things about herself

and private matters of all the family.

There were events of mine that Mama knew,

things I needed to tell her, but, only her ...

and she gave good advice to me, ...

but, ... at the family dinner table,

to my shame,

she revealed what was privately mine to keep.

There was no need to protest, I came to learn;

Mama's way always won.

There were other things that happened

that confused my brain, ...

that made reason and emotions spin.

Some other day, I may tell you of them.

I've never had an intimate friendship

because Mama taught me that I shouldn't trust.

I don't trust completely because even Mama betrayed me.
For most of my life, I've been conflicted
between trusting her because she was my mother
and not trusting her because experience taught me better.
There was a great chasm for years
as I dropped one by one, her philosophies.
We both missed that dear companionship
that we'd had so many years,
which for the most part were delightful days.
Mama taught me many valuable lessons
that I've used throughout my life,
but, I had to become the master of my days
and sort out what was right of those ways.
Mama never did understand what was wrong ...
or ... she just chose to sing the same old song.
I wanted to come to a new understanding,
but, the struggle with Mama was useless.
Before her life ended, I let that cause go.
Mama was not going to change;
she was the only way she knew and chose to be.
Mama's way had worked for her all of her life;
she found no cause to change.
All I could change was me.

I could, perhaps, have turned my back,

but, that wouldn't have ended my bad memories.

The only option that was acceptable to me was to let Mama be Mama.

I had to forgive her and just let her be.

It didn't go smoothly even those last years;

I was emotionally duped and manipulated.

Whether intentionally or innocently, I'll probably never know,

but, that doesn't matter now.

When I stopped trying to change Mama's ways,

I began to see her life and understand.

Things happened when she was a child

that consumed her with determination

to control her life, her home, her family ... beautifully.

In the adversity of illness and old age, Mama lost most of her control.

In her waning days, Mama looked to God for a purpose for her soul

and she became beautiful in her loving and giving.

"I forgive you, Mama, for those times you didn't love me well.

You were the best you knew how to be.

No mother knows how to mother her child, ...

certainly,

not perfectly."

+g

A Happy Ending

If you would have your story be happily ended, ...

let there be courage, ... forgiveness,

and tears well spent, ...

good thoughts in your heart and your words well-meant.

Let your prayers to God in glorious faith be sent.

Though treasured times

have come and gone,

other jewels will come along.

Remember those joys of yesterday

and give them to whom you love today.

Fill your dreams through the night

with love and soft moonlight, ...

and your daytimes with charity, ...

labor, ... and laughter.

Turn loose the regrets in your history.

Hold fast to the blessings of life today, ...

today, ...

tomorrow, ...

and everyday!

+g

Early April Kansas Prairies

I looked today upon a time and beauty so precious
that I wanted to drink it all into my heart
and keep it with me forever.
It is spring again,
early April on the Kansas prairies.
The restless earth keeps changing.
I want to get my fill of the treasures here before me,
for it seems to be here only a moment
before a new scene takes it's place.
I love to listen to the tranquil silence,
filled with noisy meadowlark's songs and
the percussion of a hundred small green frogs
down by the fishing pond.
I sense something spiritual in this earth.
There is something that is unchanging
from the centuries gone by
to the centuries that I assume will be.
It's stable and unchanging,
yet, it's never standing still.
It is holding buried treasures
of peoples and times gone past,

yet, it's alive and grasping the now
as though it forever would.
I turned my eyes to the bright blue sky,
after the rain was over
and watched the out-of-reach clouds,
like fantasies skip across the race of time.
I visioned them so like my dreams
that may or may not come true.
Grief comes one sad moment for any soul
that has not heard these songs
nor seen grass wet with dew.
Stretching out before me
on the early April Kansas prairies,
are puddles of daisies glowing after the rain, ...
blue daisies, so blue they hint of purple.
They lay low over the grass
next to pools of white ones,
little prairie daisies
with crowns of vivid gold.
Bright yellow dandelions splash sun here and there,
and if you look closely,
you'll find more hidden there.

Tiny Johnny-Jump-Ups, like blue pansies, pale,

blend into the grass like mist in a vale.

Frothy white sand plum thickets

shelter brown-eyed cotton-tails.

They'll be touched by gentle butterflies

when the sun is glowing warm.

The winter's naked cottonwoods are wakened.

They stretch their rough and rugged arms.

Their fingers praise the heavens

with jewels of waxened charms.

On the early April Kansas prairie,

just feel the promise

in that freshly showered breeze.

My heart leaps!

My life runs!

My spirit rings!

My soul bows to it's knees.

+g

April, 1985, by Gloria Faye Reida Coykendall

She Is Strong

Her name holds the meaning of her life and soul.

These things can only be according to the Lord

through his gift of free will that He gave to each and all.

Our granddaughter's name is Meleah Faye.

Meleah, taken from the lineage of Jesus Christ,

is unknown to us except that He was remembered

by Bible record for all time, a place of dignity.

Faye is another word form for faith.

It is an essential spiritual gift

for the gain of eternal salvation.

By the grace of God, my granddaughter has come through

sorrows, pain, confusion, and trials.

She is living proof of the truth in God's Word,

Romans 8:28.

She has become strong, not tossed to and fro

by the changing of the winds.

If the ancestor of Jesus was like this namesake,

I imagine him to be of strong faith and character,

because, for Meleah, a strong spirit

is what God has made of her.

+g

David, Our Grandson-In-Law

As grandparents, and getting older, we count ourselves blessed.

We've had the privilege to know David, a slayer of Goliaths.

He's a leader, but not the kind that's too proud to do dirty work.

Now, we weren't really happy when he married our young Leah;

we weren't ready, ... didn't at all approve of that!

Somehow the big, lovable lug, wound his way into our hearts!

David is a tornado of energy.

He always seems to be busy at his work

or helping someone in need, as needs are everywhere.

He's enthusiastically ready to do whatever he can do for you.

David's smart, has a broad knowledge of numerous things.

He's a fixer, but not a fixer only,

he's full of unexpected things of the heart.

One of his passions is his love of fine music.

He is the one we call

when we need a guy that can do the job

better than Gorilla Glue!

We admire and respect David.

If you could know him, you would, too.

+g

Faith T'A'dora

Meleah was just a girl when she read of a girl, T'A'dora.

That's the name she would give her little girl someday.

Faith T'A'dora means 'faith, the divine gift from God.'

The thought gave her heart a lift.

Our great-granddaughter is a natural performer.

Full of enthusiasm and energy, she hardly has a fear.

Almost fearless before her audience, she dances, sings,

and plays piano.

Her Daddy takes her bowling ... and coaches and cheers for his girl,

as she plays T-ball, basketball, and all athletic things, ...

and all of her endeavors in various forms of art.

She's an avid reader, a scholastic achiever.

We are Faith's great-grandparents and proud

of all her many talents, but, especially, her good behavior,

her kind and helpful ways to others.

She's a girl who seeks to know the Lord.

At her young old age of twelve, we watch her and wonder

about her unusual sense of responsibility.

What will the Lord call her to do and be?

It could be that she is already doing it!

+g

I Am

I am a girl ... in a woman's body.

I am an innocent child ... with grandchildren.

I am a maiden, ... married many years.

I am a babe in Christ in search of souls to win.

Who is this motherly woman

who cooks in the kitchen here?

Who primps her hair and shines ...

for the old man of the house?

Who is the grandma who sings to the baby ...

in yonder rocking chair?

Who is that on her knees in prayer?

Does she really care?

I am that girl, planning this and that,

and ... I am that plump little lady,

slowly growing wrinkled and old.

I am that withered, silver-haired saint, ...

yet, ... I'm still the young girl waiting

for the days of her life to unfold.

+g

Your Burden?

A great heavy burden hinders you today.

It is draining strength away.

It consumes your mind.

Your thoughts churn over and over again ...

for this problem is

the seriously destructive kind.

You cry, ... you feel sick,

desperately hoping that

some bit of wisdom you may find.

This is no sudden trouble

that has come upon you.

It's been growing and threatening you

and your loved ones, too,

day after day and week after week.

You fear your fears will come true.

You are overwhelmed by it.

What can you do?

Can you do anything? ...

today, I mean?

If there's nothing you can do about it

that is constructive today,

then you're wasting this day

by worrying it away.

Focus your mind on some good thing to do

and step away from that problem.

Breathe deeply and go outdoors.

Watch the clouds drift in blue.

Some other day when the time is right,

the answer will come to you

or

leave it alone

for God to do.

+g

From Their Father's Heart
Part One: My Prodigal Son

"Oh, My Darling Son, please don't go away!

It will break my heart if you don't stay.

Honor thy father and mother, too;

a longer life it will give to you.

We love you, Dear Son, and we pray for you ...

that God will bless you all your life through.

Don't turn away from your God up above.

Don't leave your home and the people you love.

There's a world out there that is fickle and mean.

They'll take all you have with a greed you've not seen.

Though their ways seem more fun than our lives of hard labor,

there'll be a time come when your home, you will savor.

Though I beg with my heart for you to stay,

I will not prevent you from going your way.

God gave the right to each to choose;

I'll not take that from you ... although much you will lose."

"Now you are gone and I don't know where.

The time is so long for this grief I bear.

I pray to God to forgive your sin;

I pray you'll come safely home again."

I look down the road so far away, ...
"Oh, make it soon for I'm turning gray.
Your brother's my comforter; I love him dearly.
Attentive and constant, he's precious to me,
but, he is one ... and you are another;
he can't fill the place in my heart for his brother.
Though you've gone wrong, ... I still want and I long;
Come again, come again, to this home you belong!"

I see a far traveler coming down the road, ...
weary and heart-sick from the weight of his load.
We'll welcome him here, give him drink, give him meat,
and a place to sit down to rest his feet.
Who could he be?
From where did he come?
The form looks familiar; could it be my son?
The very thought! My heart skips a beat!
I race down the path! Will a stranger I meet?
No! It is my son! It's my son that I greet!
"Oh, I praise Thee, Lord. Thy mercy is sweet."

"My Son, My Son, you've come home at last!

Rest in my arms. Forget the past.

Yes, I know you regret that you caused me sorrow.

I do forgive you.

Now, let's look to tomorrow!

You wish to be a servant to me???

Oh, no, My Son! You're forgiven and free!

Put on this ring and this garment of blue.

Our people will come!

Yes! Quite a few!

A celebration, we'll have for you,

as, also, the angels of heaven do!"

Part Two: My Faithful Son

My Dear Son, you have stayed by my side each day

through the sweet and the bitter,

you stayed, what may.

Through winter's cold and summer's heat,

we worked side by side, the challenge to meet.

We have wept together

when we felt we we're beat

and we've laughed together over victories, sweet.

I may never give you a ring of gold, ...

I may never kill a fatted calf, ...

to call all our friends in your behalf,

but, I've loved you, My Son, each and every day;

I've given you myself as we went our way.

I will love you always ...

and, likewise, your brother.

Please don't envy the things that I give the other.

Your brother has not the things I gave you.

My days with him have been shortened and few.

Require not your brother for his sins to pay.

Resent not my joy at his coming today.

You've been a blessing to me;

be my blessing still.

Be my kindred heart. That is your father's will.

Not only my sorrows, but, share my joy, too.

Love me; ...

love your brother, ...

as I love you.

+g

April, 1989, Gloria Faye Reida Coykendall

Yesterday, Today, Or Tomorrow

Will today be what you want it to be
while you brood over mistakes
that can't be undone?
Shall today be what you'd like it to be
while you focus on things
that haven't yet come?
Hold your thoughts to this day;
don't relive by-gone sorrows.
Hold your thoughts to this day;
and die not from fear of troubled tomorrows.
Live well this day;
diminish yesterday's sorrow.
Pave the way each day to a brighter tomorrow.
It's a fresh new day;
Hold each moment dearly to your heart.

+g

Why?

A world without color, what would it be like to live there?

Do we eat color, drink it, breathe it?

Is it shelter from the elements? ...the rain, cold, and heat?

Do we actually need it? If so, why? I don't know.

I do know I love these glorious arrays of color.

If the world would turn gray, I don't think I could bear to be here.

Infinite shades of color! See!

Colors are in the sun, the moon, the stars! ...

in the emerald green pastures and the blue-green seas!

As though the number of colors were too small,

the seasons change and bring with them a new array of colors;

something new for winter, spring, summer, and fall, ...

soft to bright and dark to light, ...

beautiful, mysterious, glorious colors!

I'm thankful that I can see.

Surely, color is a gift to us, ...

from The Creator, ... a gift from His grace.

Colors give me joy ...

and sometimes 'me thinks'

they heal me!

+g

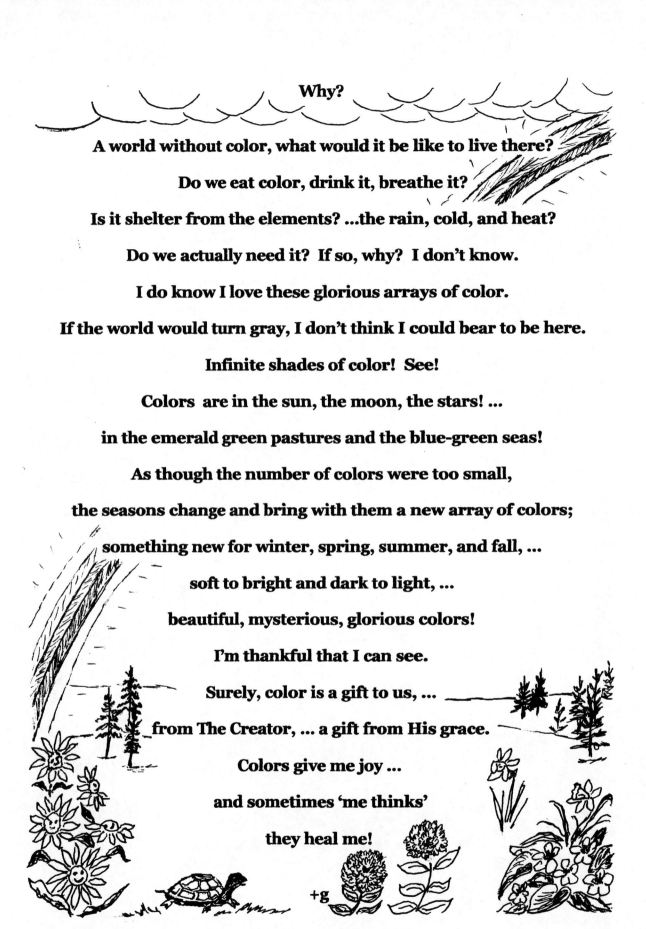

The Beautiful Snow

The snow softly fell through the soft gray day ...
and all night long, as in beds we lay.
When this morning we woke from our cozy warm night;
our hearts leaped with joy at the beautiful sight!
Daddy was grumpy, ... must be something he ate;
don't know why he won't look at this snow that's so great!
Everything that's in sight is covered with snow, ...
and the sun, as it's rising, just makes it all glow!
All the world is clean and sparkling white; ...
a miracle of God, heaped high through the night.
Mama likes to bake on a day such as this;
Our kitchen's good smell will be heavenly bliss.
We'll get a dishpan full of clean white snow ...
before we tumble and make tracks where we go.
We'll help Mama turn the snow to ice cream; ...
vanilla, ... eggs, ... sugar, ... it's a yummy dream!
Daddy will like the ice cream we make.
We'll stand 'round the fire if we shiver and shake.
'Though Daddy's feet, hands, and nose are cold,
the warmth of his heart could never be told.
When he comes indoors from the cold and snow,...

we'll hug him and kiss him; how his eyes will glow!
After steamy hot cocoa and Mama's warm buttered bread, ...
again, we'll be snuggled down deep in our bed, ...
but, we must look outdoors at the night 'fore we go ...
at the sparkling stars in the beautiful snow.

By Gloria Faye Reida Coykendall   1989

Ecclesiastes 5

Aaahhh! It's time to eat!

Let's go to the table.

My wife has prepared it the best she is able.

Each little bit passes the test;

Our food and drink are among the best.

In a common ordinary work,

I'm just a simple man,

yet, I feel a satisfaction

in doing the best I can.

It is my decision, whatever I do!

I'll enjoy each new work

'till my days are through.

Abundance of joy will be my good health,

and even, at present, my cup is so full, ...

I've no cause in this life

to be sorrowful.

Why do I enjoy whatever I do?

I'm certainly not more perfect than you.

How can I be satisfied where ever I am?

It's a gift from God,

The Great I Am.

This blessing is great,

but, yet, comes another;

as my human life shortens,

more joy comes in my Father.

+g

Early April

Kansas prairie,

restless and changing, ...

noisy silence, ...

earth, unchanging, ...

never standing still,

hiding treasures of the past,

grasping now forever.

Clouds of fancy, ...

visions of dreams, ...

grief for life, ...

that died too new.

Puddles of daisies, ...

the glow after rain, ...

blue daisies, so blue, ...

they hint of purple, ...

laying low over the grass,

next to pools of white ones, ...

little prairie daisies, ...

with

centered crowns of vivid gold, ...

bright yellow dandelions

splash sun here and there.

Look close!

You'll see even more hidden there, ...

Johnny-Jump-Ups, like blue pansies, pale,

blended into the grasses

like mist in the vale.

Frothy sand plum thickets that shelter

brown-eyed cottontails.

The winter's naked cottonwoods awake

and stretch out their arms

to feel the promise in the showered breeze.

Hearts leap, ...

life runs, ...

and spirits ring ...

out on the Kansas prairie, ...

early April.

Elevator Up!

"I'll meet you here at four. We'll do the museum before we eat supper."

"What time do you have?" asked Dan, "I have 2:05."

"Mine is the same."

Concerned, Dan stated, "I'm not sure you should go alone. Are you sure you know how to get there?"

"Yes, I'll be fine. It's as safe here as our own hometown. It is broad daylight and I won't do anything that I think risky."

Reluctantly, Dan turned to go. "Four sharp! Mark and I will do our shopping and meet you here."

My shoes must have been made with springs in the soles; it felt as though I were prancing across the shining mall floor, crossing the paths of shoppers.

They were strangers, yet kindred faces, .. young, old, and middle-aged. Each face carried a unique story behind it of the life they had led, the people they loved, and the enemies that they had fought.

The pleasant buzzing of the customers filled my ears with music of the living. Glorious rays of sun beamed through the skylights above me. I felt light and carefree, ... tall, ... beautiful, ... and healthy!

This family vacation had been a beautiful one. I'd never enjoyed traveling and sight-seeing quite as much as I had on this trip.

Now each of us had separate ways to go for a few individual wants. It would be a break from one another for a couple of hours. When we'd meet again, we would be refreshed and more companionable for the last day of our week together.

Happily, I thought about how glad I was that Mama's health had improved so much. Now she was busy and interested in people and things outside of her house once again. For a long time, she had been depressed and confined with one illness after another.

Buddy and his family were harvesting wheat by now. I was hoping they would not have machinery break-downs to slow their summer work.

My grown children were running through my mind, just wondering what they were doing. Christy would be busy with her little ones or maybe, chattering and laughing as they browsed through treasures at a yard sale. She loves going to yard sales and flea markets.

It's hard to believe she is the same girl that seemed so hopelessly caught in the drug scene a few years ago. At that time, I didn't think she would still be living today. How wonderful it is to have her back and …. with two more lovely little girls!

"Thank You, Father!"

Kirk's wife, Bonnie, would be watching our frisky little tom-boy, Deanna, and trying to do dishes or something. She is starting to show. She's probably daydreaming about having a boy so she can call off having more babies. She would like to teach school again someday when the babies don't need as much attention from her.

Kirk would still be in his office, absorbed in challenging work. He likes a challenge, but later, on the drive home, he might daydream of running a children's camp.

He says, "God seems to have given me a heart and the athletic skills to do activities outdoors with kids, but, He hasn't shown me a way to do it! Why?"

Where, oh, where would Kendall be? I hope he is alright. He hasn't put down roots anywhere. I think he feels uprooted! He talks a bit about Arizona, but hasn't done anything. Maybe it's finances.

Through much of his youth, Kendall has been in trouble. I wish it would stop. I wish so much for him. He has a good heart. It's getting late in life for him to make the changes, but miracles do happen.

I don't know if I could have done better by Kendall or not, having been a very young mother when he was born. In trying to avoid doing the wrong thing again, I refused the favor that he asked when he was in distress, now he sees me as his enemy.

It's been a long bad dream, but, there's nothing more I can do now. Strangely, I do not feel any fears about Kendall's future. I guess I have finally let go of him to let he and God work out those problems.

Perhaps, it would have been to everyone's good if I had taken my meddling hands off my older children's lives years ago. Somehow, I thought it was my business to fix the problems for my family, but it seldom helped. I should have trusted matters to God sooner.

For one who was feeling so light and free, an awful lot went whizzing through my mind in a matter of minutes!

It was an unexpected surprise to have Mark free to come with us on this trip. We've had many old traveling stories to retell as we zoomed down the highway in our Mini.

Mark had the future spinning in his head. He plans for us to drop him off to meet his friend, Kenny, in California. They can hardly wait for the group to get together to work up the new songs. They're ready to go full steam into performing and recording their music. Goodness! Such Big Dreams!

Previously, Mark seemed to be getting comfortable at his office job. He learned a lot about business and the public through that work. He had nice people to work with and they seemed to like him. They were satisfied with his work, but Mark had an opportunity to move toward his dreams of a career in music.

Thankful thoughts for the blessings God has been sending strengthen my hopes for all my loved ones. I'm expecting good things! None of these dreams could have ever come true, if God had not made it possible. I feel that God gave the grace to my darling Dan and I to make it through the rocky years of our marriage, ... and surely that had a helpful effect on the whole family. We had our times when we didn't suppose we could hold ourselves together.

Sweet man that my husband is, ... what a time we had! Marriage is not an easy thing. Some days, I thought things couldn't get worse, but, then, ... they would! Only God gets the credit for pulling us through the gloom, into the light, into happy days. Even during our conflicts, we still cared about one another!

We've learned a lot. We've changed. We remember those 'people' and can tell their stories, but, we feel like we are different people now.

People say, "Oh, to be young again!" ... and I agree that there is something about youth that is charged with adventure. There is, also, a great deal of pain, guilt, fears, and self-pity, ... very destructive things going on in the brain and emotions. At least, that's the way I remember it!

Our mature years are proving more rewarding for Dan and me. We now listen more sensitively to one another's thoughts. We are more careful to be considerate. The fragility of life has persuaded us to take better advantage of the good qualities that we find in our present moments.

Life is good. The expectation of good things to come just fills me up and flows over the edge of my cup! There are so many things I want to do. There are so many missions to fill.

I will confess that I have a tendency to get anxious because of my impatience to do everything now before it gets too late. Depression does slip up on me when I get overwhelmed with things undone.

"Watch it, Faye! Keep your focus on the now! No good comes from dwelling on either the past or future. All that can be done is take care of now."

My RV neighbor told me last night that there was a wonderful arts and crafts shop on the third or fourth floor of the building across the street. I'd better hurry so I'll have time to look at the creative ideas that people have!

Gracious! This building is huge! It looks so old. The dark stone exterior has an occasional spot of green lichen-like moss in the niches. The architecture is so massive compared to buildings built today. I wonder when on earth this towering building was built!

Inside, the first floor was ablaze with light. I had to stand a moment, scanning the layout of the place, ... looking for the way to the upper floors.

There's the elevator. It is massive, too!

As I waited, I studied the frame and the doors, which appeared to be made of heavy brass, ... deeply designed and tarnished dark greenish-brown except where it was polished bright by frequent use.

("Ho! Ho! Have I just hit on a parable? ... A Christian's Christianity only shines where it is well used! Hmmmm, not a bad insight.)

I'm thinking I'd better figure out how to get on this thing if I want to get up to that art show. Elevators always make me a little nervous and this one is so big, ... so different, ... and SO OLD!

Maybe someone else will come along to go upstairs with me. Then, I hope the door doesn't start to close before I can get through it!

The great doors opened smoothly. A tall white-haired attendant was dressed in a simple robe of deep wine velvet. He announced, "Elevator up!"

"Well, I made it," I thought to myself. I leaned against the back wall, taking in my surroundings.

The interior was as unique as the exterior. The shadowy interior was lit from high above us. The light looked like a large blue-white star, ... far, far away. THE ELEVATOR HAD NO CEILING!!!

There were only a few other passengers and the attendant. We stood around the walls, facing one another, ... pleasantly, but, silently. I had an eery feeling that there was something here that did not meet the eye.

"Why," I wondered, "is this elevator built so large? It's bigger than my kitchen, but not many people in it."

The attendant stood silently opposite of me, but had not made any eye contact. The doors were shut and I could feel the thing moving upward, but there were no controls beside the man, ... and ... I had not been asked what floor I wanted!

"Floor?" There was no floor indicator above the doors, "What is this place? I've made a mistake. How do I get off?"

"Excuse me, Sir. Would you let me out at the next floor, please?"

The attendant, in velvet robe, turned his eyes to mine as I spoke to him. His calm expression told me neither 'Yes' or 'No.' He made no reply. The man's face showed no intent to do me harm so I lay that fear to rest, but, ... inside my quandary was beginning to overwhelm me.

"Don't make a scene! Don't lose control of your senses! There's a simple explanation that will soon become obvious."

Inwardly, my thoughts were churning. Outwardly, I stood perfectly still.

"Is this the worst nightmare that I've ever had? ... or ... am I lost? ... or trapped? Whatever this is, I think I may never be able to go back ... to where I have lived."

My concern turned to Dan and Mark. I wondered what they were doing at this moment, ... and what will they think has happened to me when I don't meet them at four? How long will they search for me before they give up?

"Oh, I cannot stand to leave them! It is too painful to think of their anguish, their unanswered questions. I hurt more for them than I fear for myself!"

"Get control of yourself, Faye! You are being unreasonable! The elevator will stop soon. You'll walk off and see reality again. All of this is a trick of the imagination. For some unexplainable reason, you've temporarily lost control of your thoughts and feelings."

"Of course! I'm alright now. I know the elevator will stop soon. We should be almost to the top floor. We've been going up for quite a while and we seem to be increasing in speed. There has been no intermediate stop for another level! WHY?"

"What a ride! We started at the ground floor and are zooming right to the top!"

"When I get off, I'll go to the stairs and start down immediately! Perhaps, I can make it in time to meet the guys. Whatever! I don't plan to take the elevator again!"

"Good grief! Is this thing ever going to stop? I need to be getting back to my family! We need to be together. It's too frightening to get separated from my family in a strange city. What will I do?"

"Have I lost my mind? Will I travel this imaginary machine, ... lost in space and time forever?"

I felt great relief and sane once again when the elevator began slowing ... and ... finally, it came to a gentle stop.

The doors were opening. "Oh, thank You, Lord, ... I'm so exhausted and so thankful!"

As my happy legs carried me into a bright and beautiful room, I tried to assess just where I was.

It was surely an auditorium because there were rows and rows of chairs in the mammoth room, a meeting room.

Evidently, it was not time for the meeting to begin because most of the seating was still empty. All around the room were large windows looking out at a bright blue sky with brilliantly white, soft frothy clouds.

A small group of folks were leisurely chatting with one another. I heard the elevator doors close behind me and I moved toward the group. I must get directions to the stairs so I can get back to ground floor.

The small group noticed the sound of the doors and they turned with beaming smiles, ... expectantly, ... toward me!

"Welcome! Welcome! Oh, we're so glad you've come! Praise God, it's so good to have you here with us!"

A small elderly lady rose from her chair to lead the happy faces toward me, opening her arms wide to gather me into a loving hug.

She was a sweet and simple little lady that could have been most anyone's grandma or favorite auntie. Her joy in greeting me was obviously genuine.

I was being welcomed as if this meeting was just for me! The little woman said, "Come on in, Honey. You don't be afraid because we are all Christians here and we are going to have a wonderful time!"

"Oh, that does sound wonderful! I really would like to stay if it were some other time. You see, I've been separated from my family. They will be worried and looking for me. I must go to find the rest of my family! I must get back to them!" I explained with tears spilling.

The little lady clasped my hand understandingly and looked squarely into my eyes. With a sure, clear voice, she commanded my attention. "Honey, if they are supposed to be here, then, they will be here. If some of them aren't, then you can't do anything about it now."

I knew what she meant. I had hope and I, also, accepted what she said as true, ... finally, ... knowing where I was.

I joined the group, quietly reflecting on the years I had lived. I gazed at the glorious sunshine, the beautiful blue of the skies. I was at peace in my faith, and ready to welcome the next family member, or friend, or stranger to the meeting that would soon take place.

There were a lot of chairs to be filled. That must mean that the meeting expected a good number of saved souls, (those of the people who had decided to walk with faith in God through whatever trials might come their way.)

I could do no more now to persuade those precious loved ones who were teetering on the fence between belief and disbelief, ... however, God was still speaking to their hearts!

I believe that more of my family will come. I expect my Dan, and I earnestly hope for my children, that they will all make that sure commitment before it is too late. ... AND ..... those sweet little grand babies! ... THEY will be here! Bless their hearts! +g

February, 1984, by Gloria Faye Reida Coykendall

Our Two Little Aussie Boys

One charming guy, Jye, from Australia,

charmed our sweet granddaughter, the lovely Billie Jo, ...

while they adventured in their work

in the wonderful world of the old rodeo!

And wouldn't you just know?

He swept her heart away!

She now speaks Aussie fluently, ...

'You know what I mean, aye?'

She no longer rides wild, bucking bulls, ...

but, riding herd on two lively boys.

Billie sends photos to us

by the marvelous means of computers, ...

Zac Tyler, the bright eyed five-year-old,

and his baby brother, Ethan Quinn, ...

our handsome and happy great-grandsons, ...

our two little Aussie boys!

They're so far away from old grandpa and grandma;

there ought to be a law!

We'll probably never cross the seas

to their fair country of Australia!

We'd like to see their house,
taste the foods they eat,
See them do what they do,
see their animals, their rivers, their trees.
Each night we pray
God will bless that precious family.
Daddy Jye and Mama Josie have much to do
to raise their beautiful sons, ...
so far, far away, ...
our two little Aussie boys.

+g

January, 2005, by Gloria Faye Reida Coykendall

Born Again!

So, that's what it was!
I wonder if the wonder
will stay or pass.
Will it be again
like it was back when?
Who would ever wish that to be!
Oh, please, dear God,
let this joy always remain.
Help me to always be
'BORN AGAIN!'

+g

We Love You Just As You Are

Hey, there, little guy, Tristan Ray Romero!
Welcome to the world!
You're only nine days old.
We visited you for the first time yesterday.
We will cherish that day all our years,
although, our hearts are swelled with tears
because you have a birth defect.
You will need operations as you grow
to keep you healthy physically and emotionally.
It is because doctors care for little boys like you
that they have learned how to do hard things
to fix your problem so that you'll be able
to swallow food and breathe better, too.
The doctors and nurses will know you hurt,
so they'll have good medicine to take hurt away
and get you healthy and strong really quick.
Great-grandpa says he wishes he could take all
of those operations for you.
Daddy Matt says he would like to just keep you as you are
and protect you from all pain.
We love you just as you are,

but, Tristan Ray Romero,

there are times when a fellow must do what he must do.

Mama Megan adores you,

clucking around her chick like an old mama hen!

As for now, we'll pray for you

and we'll ask our friends in other churches to pray, too.

We WILL BELIEVE in Romans 8:28,

that all things work for good

to those who love God

and are the called according to His purpose.

We plan to have more good times

as we did just yesterday.

I want to remember

the feel of your velvet newborn skin,

your softly ruffled black hair,

the sparkle of dark eyes sneaking a peak,

your artistic long fingers and the shape of your nails,

and your little great toes.

Great-grandpa and grandma wish you all that is good;

what that is, we know that God knows.

We love you just as you are!

+g

Say Farewell This Way

I don't plan to leave this world right away,

but, I have a few last wishes

I hope you'll remember someday.

Our customs change through cultures and time

and I've come to hope for things done this way.

These last wishes, I implore you;

don't take leave of your work day

or cut short the family holiday

to sit at my funeral

or stand at my graveside

to show your respect to me.

Grieve for me whenever and however you would,

for releasing your pain is good,

but, remember, please,...

your love for me cannot be proved

by gazing at my body of flesh

that lies there dead.

Let your tribute to me be during my life; ...

you've meant so much to me; ...

so, I'd be honored to be remembered

when you chat with friends over coffee or tea.

Think of me when you hear the breeze

as it whispers through the leaves of your trees.

Think of me in the sunshine

and in the song that you sing.

Think of me when the flowers bloom;

place one in your window for me.

Don't spend your hard-earned money

on a frivolous funeral array.

When you want to say 'Hello' or 'Good-bye,'

just stop by my grave when you come my way,

or

when you look into a babbling brook,

or

into the blue heavens where clouds are floating.

My grave does not require tending

nor adorning of wreaths and sprays.

If you like, bring wild yellow sunflowers

or some daisies you've picked by the way.

If you need to come there to see me

for a place to quietly pray,

rest yourself on the stone o'er my body;

sort out your thoughts for the day.

It's no sin; it's okay ... if you see me in body

as you think and you pray; ...

but, please, ...

don't worship that old flesh!

Praise God! I'm not in it today!

If my life meant something to you,

if I've helped you in any way,

pass it on while your life you are living.

Love a child.

Touch a soul.

Give each day.

Whatever you've received from me,

you must give away.

My last wishes, in love, I have given.

If you hear or not, I don't know.

I've planted the seeds

by His grace through you.

I pray what I've planted

will be fruitful and continue forever to grow.

+g

— April 8, 2003, by Gloria Faye Reida Coykendall

Bailee Nicole

Bailee Nicole, where are you?

I'm looking for you. Yooo-hooooooo!

I have a picture of a pretty little girl, ...

sitting in front of our flag, Old Glory, ...

the beautiful red, white, and blue.

She's a bright girl with sparkle in her eyes

and a winsome, gleaming smile.

Is that what makes her face shine so?

Wearing a bright red dress and hair bow, ...

age three or almost four, full of goodness from head to toe, ...

she looks like an angel all aglow!

Why, for goodness sakes! Is that you, sweet Bailee Nicole?

Well, I thought it looked like you!

Are you now older and taller and going to preschool?

Everyday, do you do something exciting?

Are you reading and writing?

Come tell us about it, ... old great grandma and grandpa!

You tell your Mama Megan that you'd like to come our way!

She will say, "Great idea, Bailee-bug! ...Let's go! Okay?"

+g

December, 2005, by Gloria Faye Reida Coykendall

Cancer

The malignancy called cancer has now come to our house!

We've felt the pain of others so stricken, ...

friends or family from far and near!

We've been aware of the devastation, ...

the shocking change for the ill one ...

and the family caught in turmoil,

anguished by the suffering of their ill,

and fearing the future where they may be alone.

They grieve for a lost way of life, ...yesterday's normal routine.

We, now, see things from a new perspective.

We appreciate small moments of laughter.

Clingingly, I memorize shared words of love.

I try to imprint his gentle face in my mind.

I resound again the sound of his voice!

I inhale his familiar scent that will, later, bring his love to me

in a moment, unexpected in time.

Save the memories! Save the memories!

They may be all that I have!

These musings must be necessary preparation,

but, no one knows, except God, the number of our days.

We wish to be with our loved ones forever and again.

We would love our days together, whole-heartedly, ...

not taking them for granted, ... not judging, criticizing,

nor trying to change one another's ways.

We would gaze into their eyes

and wipe away the tears when our loved one cries.

Now, when it's nearly too late, we want to hold onto a lifetime.

We want to erase the cruel things said and done.

Life is life and who would know until they've been there? None.

At a time like this, nothing seems good.

Mundane needs still call for attention! Why?

I know of more important matters, don't I?

I don't know how I'll cope with days ahead.

Will I die a bit each day? ...

or will I choose to carry-on with life as usual?

Will I try to cling to some semblance of normal?

Will memories come to warm my heart

and make my days glad and thankful and peaceful?

Life changes and changes and changes.

Each phase of life makes us someone else.

It's what happens to us and how we react to it that changes our form

'though we're still somewhat the same person.

So, cancer will now change us;

how depends on how we decide to meet our crisis.

Let's be prepared for death

and still expect to be healed; ... I pray we will.

Every soul has need to be prepared for death's aftermath.

Our soul's primary need is spiritual.

If we have not already done so, we need to decide who we are, ...

in relationship to ourselves, ... the greater power, ...

to God, our Heavenly Father, ...

to Sweet Holy Spirit, who is our Comforter, ...

to our Lord and Saviour, God's Son, Jesus Christ Immanuel!

Through Him, we can be ready to go through death

to what awaits on the other side of breath.

The person without cancer and the one with,

both,

must be prepared spiritually and, also, physically.

Our physical needs are part of our whole person,

so, do put your physical world in order as well as you can

and leave the rest to God.

+g

October, 2004, by Gloria Faye Reida Coykendall

God Knows Her

**God knows that little woman
'though she is plain
and has no skills quite remarkable.
Her calling from God,
'though, at nothing, she's best,
is to make herself
readily available.**

+g

June, 2000, by Gloria Faye Reida Coykendall

Young Person, God Calls

Young Person, prepare!

Your God calls you somewhere.

You may already suspect

what God wants you to do;

so, ...

prepare! Prepare! Prepare!

But, Young Person, don't wait

'till you're perfectly ready;

you may never quite make it

there.

Beware! Beware! Beware!

+g

June 17, 2000, by Gloria Faye Reida Coykendall

Encourage Me!

Oh, good neighbor, please be my good Samaritan,

for I am heartsick, down, and weary.

Have you balm for my wounded soul and body?

Oh, touch me with your healing hand and speak to me.

Encourage me!

Oh, dear loved ones, strangers, and fellow countrymen,

I feel lost, ... my future, hopelessly dreary.

Speak faith to me, speak hope! Take my hand. Help me stand.

For the love of God, encourage me!

Oh, Self, you fragile baby Christian,

take encouragement from all that's holy!

Be still, patient, and faithful. Be not down-hearted; be cheery!

The Lord is able to encourage thee.

Oh, Holy God, The Great I Am, my strength is depleted daily.

Renew my courage again, I pray.

On Thy Holy Promises, I will stand. Thank You, Father!

I am blessed again ...

because ... you did encourage me!

Amen

+g

January, 2005, by Gloria Faye Reida Coykendall

Of What Worth Is A Seed?

A few apple seeds I hold in my hand;

it seems too little to do anything grand.

I can count them as less than my ten fingers.

Why bother to plant? My question lingers.

I laid them aside, found another chore,

kept myself busy, thought about them no more.

God's Holy Spirit came, gave me a directive

to see those seeds from His perspective.

"In each tiny seed is a tree and its fruit.

You plant what you have. Get busy! Do it!

And... I have given you seeds of another kind;

set them foremost in your heart and mind.

Prepare a soul's soil; in it, sow the seed.

Water it faithfully.

Pull out weed after weed.

In faith and in love,

sow where you go;

these small God seeds

produce more than you know!"

+g

ISBN 1412027B5-3